Self-Paced Phonics

Self-Paced Phonics:
A Text for Educators

Fifth Edition

Roger S. Dow
Frostburg State University

G. Thomas Baer
Illinois State University

PEARSON

Boston Columbus Indianapolis New York San Francisco Upper Saddle River
Amsterdam Cape Town Dubai London Madrid Milan Munich Paris Montréal Toronto
Delhi Mexico City São Paulo Sydney Hong Kong Seoul Singapore Taipei Tokyo

Associate Sponsoring Editor: Barbara Strickland
Vice President, Editor-in-Chief: Aurora Martínez Ramos
Editorial Assistant: Michelle Hochberg
Marketing Manager: Krista Clark
Production Editor: Mary Beth Finch
Editorial Production Service: Element LLC
Manufacturing Buyer: Megan Cochran
Electronic Composition: Element LLC
Cover Designer: Jennifer Hart

Library of Congress Cataloging-in-Publication Data
Dow, Roger S.
  Self-paced phonics : a text for educators / Roger S. Dow, G. Thomas Baer.—5th ed.
    p. cm.
Includes bibliographical references.
ISBN-13: 978-0-13-288367-2
ISBN-10: 0-13-288367-8
1. Reading—Phonetic method. 2. Reading (Elementary) I. Baer, G. Thomas. II. Title.
LB1573.3.B34 2013
372.46'5—dc23

                      2011036774

10 9 8 7 6 5 4 3 2 1 [EDW] 15 14 13 12

www.pearsonhighered.com

ISBN-10: 0-13-288367-8
ISBN-13: 978-013-288367-2

About the Authors

Dr. Roger S. Dow is Director of the Reading Clinic and the Graduate Reading Program at Frostburg State University where he has taught for over 30 years. Prior to coming to Frostburg, Dr. Dow received his Ph.D. from The Ohio State University in reading and in psychology. He is an active member of the International Reading Association, with varied interests in linguistics and foreign languages as they relate to English.

Dr. G. Thomas Baer is Emeritus Professor in the Department of Curriculum and Instruction at Illinois State University where he has taught for over 35 years. During his tenure, he has served as Elementary Education Coordinator, Department Chair, and instructor of elementary education courses specializing in reading instruction.

Contents

Preface xi

1 Introduction 1
Chapter 1: Practice 6
Points to Ponder: An Invitation to Dialogue 8

2 Phonics Pretest 9
Matching 9
True-False 10
Multiple Choice 10
Chapter 2: Practice 16
Cumulative Review: Chapters 1 and 2 17

3 Phonics Vocabulary and Phonemes 19
Vocabulary 19
Phonemes 22
  Consonant Phonemes—Pronunciation Key 22
  Vowel Phonemes—Pronunciation Key 23
Chapter 3: Practice 24
Cumulative Review: Chapters 1 to 3 28
Points to Ponder: An Invitation to Dialogue 31

4 Emergent Literacy and Phonics 32
Oral Language 33
Phonemic Awareness 35
Letter Names 38
Vision 38
Hearing 39
Visual Discrimination 40
  Visual Discrimination Exercises 40
Auditory Discrimination 41
  Auditory Awareness Exercises 41
  Auditory Discrimination Exercises 42
Chapter 4: Practice 43

Cumulative Review: Chapters 1 to 4   44
Points to Ponder: An Invitation to Dialogue   47

5 Phonic Generalizations   48

The Teaching Context of the Phonics Generalizations   49
Accurately Hearing Speech Sounds is Important   49
The Age When Second Language Learning Occurs Matters   50
Language and Culture Are Significantly Intertwined   50
Cross-Language Transfer   51
Phonics Instruction That Works   51
Consonant Generalizations   52
Vowel Generalizations   53
Chapter 5: Practice   54
Cumulative Review Chapters 1 to 5   57
Points to Ponder: An Invitation to Dialogue   58

6 Teaching Consonants and Vowels   59

Consonants   60
  Single Consonants   61
  Double C and Double G   62
  Consonant Blends (Clusters)   62
  Consonant Digraphs   63
Vowels   64
  Short–Long Vowel Sounds   65
  Vowel Digraphs   66
  R-Controlled Vowels   66
  Intrusive L and R Sounds   67
  The Schwa Sound   67
  Teaching Vowels Through Phonograms   67
Chapter 6: Practice   68
Cumulative Review: Chapters 1 to 6   70
Points to Ponder: An Invitation to Dialogue   73

7 Syllabication and Accenting   74

Chapter 7: Practice   77
Cumulative Review: Chapters 1 to 7   78
Points to Ponder: An Invitation to Dialogue   82

8 Diagnostic Teaching   83

General Principles of Diagnosis   83
Procedures for Diagnosing Phonic Skills   85
  Observation   85
  Informal Reading Inventory   85
  Diagnosis and Remediation in the Multilingual Classroom   87
  Phonemic Awareness   89

Letter Names   89
Consonant Sounds   90
Vowel Sounds   92
Conclusion   94
Chapter 8: Practice   94
Cumulative Review: Chapters 1 to 8   96
Points to Ponder: An Invitation to Dialogue   99

9   Phonics Posttest   100
Fill in the Blanks   100
True-False   101
Multiple Choice   101
Matching   106

Appendix: Answer Key   108

Glossary   129

References   132

Additional Web-based and Other Resources   144

Preface

NEW TO THIS EDITION

- Since the publication of the fourth edition of this text, the demographics of the United States have changed dramatically. Classroom teachers are now faced with the challenges and opportunities represented by multilingual classrooms. Substantive research on the impact of these demographic changes and their influence on reading instruction, especially phonics, has been added to this edition. The bibliography now includes a wider array of both national and international peer-reviewed research studies drawn from diverse academic disciplines related to and supportive of reading instruction as it relates to social change manifested in the classroom.
- Changes in federal policy initiatives related to the *No Child Left Behind Act* and its successor, *Race to the Top*, necessitated a complete review of the research base supporting this edition. Each of the original references was vetted for currency, accuracy, and appropriateness, with substantial additional references made throughout the text that substantiate the theoretical and practical aspects of the book. This edition contains more than 100 new references.
- This edition also includes substantial additions to its glossary, chapter practice items, cumulative chapter reviews, and both pre- and posttests, as a result of increased understanding in the field of reading and on changes in educational emphasis related to phonics instruction. The intent of these additions is to provide readers an easily accessible reference guide to terminology related to phonics as well as other related topics found in the text related to teaching reading in the multilingual classroom.
- To assist both preservice and practicing teachers in becoming more effective with the diverse needs of learners in their classrooms, an annotated list of professional organizations related to the teaching of phonics and to the teaching of cultural and multilingual education as they relate to teaching reading and phonics is included in this edition.
- Additional helpful Internet resources related to better understanding phonics and its daily applications in teaching have also been added. Many of these new web resources reflect the direction suggested by the research that

guided the preparation of this edition and parallel and complement the key concepts readers will encounter in their study of the text. Since the last edition, many excellent free websites supporting the teaching of phonics have been developed.

- Collaborative discussion topics for both classroom and online use have been added in each chapter, called *Points to Ponder: An Invitation to Dialogue.* The intent of this process is to encourage users of the text to delve more deeply into the substance and subjects of each chapter by sharing their perceptions and practical experiences in teaching phonics with others. This is especially important in the areas of the text that discuss multilingual education and the responses to the needs of second language learners in the classroom. While the text still provides extensive individual and self-guided opportunities to master the topics included in the study of phonics, the discussion thread component is meant to broaden learners' perspectives and allow them to target and reflect on their own values about critical topics in phonics and language learning.

Although phonics has been with us in one form or another from colonial times to the present, it continues to head the list of reading topics that elicit the most emotional responses from detractors both within and outside the teaching profession. Based on the conclusions of reports such as *Becoming a Nation of Readers: The Report of the Commission of Reading* (Anderson, Hiebert, Scott, & Wilkinson, 1984) and *Beginning to Read: Thinking and Learning About Print* (Adams, 1990), there is strong evidence to suggest that children who are taught phonics at the beginning stages of reading instruction do better than those who are not. Clearly, the question regarding phonics instruction no longer appears to be whether it should be included in beginning instruction; instead, the essential question is one of determining how phonics can be taught most effectively.

The purpose of this text is to provide preservice and practicing teachers with instruction that will assist them in developing a sound understanding of both the content and pedagogy of phonics. This instruction is accomplished through the following text features and concepts.

Meaningful practice and feedback.

- The text uses sound learning principles by providing students with meaningful practice and immediate feedback. The chapter practices, cumulative reviews, pretest, and posttest provide students with numerous opportunities to work with the content of phonics.

Self-regulating, self-monitoring learning.

- Educators will be able to complete the text with a minimal amount of direct instruction. With little formal instruction required, faculty who already face content overload will find the text teacher friendly and immediately applicable to web-based instructional models.

Complementary to reading methods.

- The text is designed to complement developmental reading methods textbooks that typically cover phonics in a superficial manner.

Phonics instruction in context.

- The text recognizes that although phonics is only one of several word recognition techniques, it remains the one that is least understood by practicing teachers.

Input from students who used the text over 6 years, along with evaluative feedback from reading professionals in the field, were used to expand and strengthen the second and third editions of this text. The fourth edition introduced web links for further exploration of phonics-related topics. It also included a source for standard pronunciation and additional information on many of the topics included in the text. This edition presents more examples that illustrate particular phonics elements and expands significantly the practices and cumulative reviews so that they provide increased opportunities for students to work with both the content and pedagogy of phonics.

ACKNOWLEDGEMENTS

Revisions for this fifth edition could not have been accomplished without the substantive assistance of the research staff at Frostburg State University, especially Pamela S. Williams and Dr. Sean Henry who generously provided their time and considerable talent in helping me navigate the intricacies of the university's research portal. I would also like to thank my graduate reading students who made countless suggestions regarding changes to the text to better facilitate their learning. I appreciate the suggestions made by the reviewers of this edition: Ann Cunniff Casey, St. Bonaventure University; Sandra Goetze, Oklahoma State University; Melinda Miller, Sam Houston State University; and Nancy Walker, University of LaVerne. Finally, I want to thank my coauthor, Dr. G. Thomas Baer, for all the preceding work this text represents.

1 Introduction

Phonics instruction has long been a controversial matter. Emans (1968) points out that the emphasis on phonics instruction has changed several times over the past two centuries. Instruction has shifted from one extreme—no phonics instruction—to the other—phonics instruction as the major method of word-recognition instruction—and back again. Emans also points out that "each time that phonics has been returned to the classroom, it usually has been revised into something quite different from what it was when it was discarded" (p. 607). Currently, most beginning reading programs include a significant component of phonics instruction. This is especially true since the implementation of policies related to the No Child Left Behind Act and recommendations by the National Reading Panel (2000) for the use of both instruction and assessments related to explicit phonics instruction. It is also likely that the U.S. Department of Education's initiative Race to the Top, funded as part of the Education Recovery Act of the American Recovery and Reinvestment Act of 2009 (AARA), will continue to view phonics instruction as an integral component and focus of reading instruction.

Phonics, however, is not the cure-all for reading ills that some believe it to be. Rudolph Flesch's book *Why Johnny Can't Read* (1955), although it did bring the phonics debate to the attention of the public, typifies the kind of literature that takes a naive approach to a complex problem. As Heilman (1981) points out, "Flesch's suggestions for teaching were quite primitive, consisting primarily of lists of words each presenting different letter-sound patterns. Thus, Flesch did not actually provide teaching materials that schools and teachers could use" (p. 3). Still, this kind of approach, which reduced learning to read to the simple task of memorizing the alphabet and learning its letter-to-sound correspondences through an emphasis on writing, attracted disciples who vigorously carried forth its message.

Teachers must remember that phonics is but one of the major word-recognition methods that also include whole-word methodology and is most effective when it includes skills of contextual analysis, structural analysis, and dictionary use. These methods do not conflict with one another. If one is a proponent of phonics instruction, one does not have to be opposed to learning words via other word-recognition methods. Rather, it should be the goal of reading teachers to develop children's skills in all these methods for three basic reasons:

1. Children will find some methods more suited to their abilities and learning styles than others. Research has consistently shown that no one method is

best for teaching all children. Thus, each child should be given opportunities to learn and use all word-recognition methods, applying those that work the most effectively for them.

2. Some words are learned more easily by using one method instead of another. For example, it may be more effective to teach an irregularly spelled word through a whole-word emphasis rather than a phonics emphasis. Focusing on word histories—the etymology of difficult words adopted from foreign languages—allows the learner to make deeper connections between the unique usage of the word and its irregular spelling.

3. When children encounter unknown words, they often use the various word-recognition techniques in concert, not as isolated skills having no relationship to one another.

Over the past 35 years, several studies and reports on reading stand out as having made major impacts on present-day phonics instruction. The first-grade reading studies (Bond & Dykstra, 1967) completed during the 1964–1965 school year provided data that have had an important and lasting influence on today's reading materials. Although the data seemed to indicate that no one method of teaching reading was superior to all others, they did suggest that an earlier and increased emphasis on phonics instruction would strengthen basal reading programs.

After an extensive critical analysis of research that examined the various approaches to beginning reading, Chall (1967) came to the following conclusions:

> My review of the research from the laboratory, the classroom, and the clinic points to the need for a correction in beginning reading instructional methods. Most schoolchildren in the United States are taught to read by what I have termed a meaning emphasis method. Yet, the research from 1912 to 1965 indicates that a code-emphasis method—i.e., one that views beginning reading as essentially different from mature reading and emphasizes learning of the printed code for the spoken language—produces better results, at least up to the point where sufficient evidence seems to be available, the end of the third grade.
>
> The results are better, not only in terms of the mechanical aspects of literacy alone, as was once supposed, but also in terms of the ultimate goals of reading instruction—comprehension and possibly even speed of reading. The long-existing fear that an initial code emphasis produces readers who do not read for meaning or with enjoyment is unfounded. On the contrary, the evidence indicates that better results in terms of reading for meaning are achieved with the programs that emphasize code at the start than with the programs that stress meaning at the beginning. (p. 307)

The National Academy of Education's Commission on Education and Public Policy, with the sponsorship of the National Institute of Education, established the Commission on Reading in 1983 to "locate topics on which there has been appreciable research and scholarship . . . and gather panels of experts from within the Academy and elsewhere to survey, interpret and synthesize research findings" (Anderson, Hiebert, Scott, & Wilkinson, 1984, p. viii).

The Commission on Reading's efforts resulted in the influential report titled *Becoming a Nation of Readers.* In the foreword to this report, Robert Glaser, president of the National Academy of Education, writes,

> The last two decades of research and scholarship on reading, building on the past, have produced an array of information which is unparalleled in its understanding of the underlying processes in the comprehension of language. Although reading abilities and disabilities require further investigation, present knowledge, combined with the centrality of literacy in the educational process, make the report cause for optimism. Gains from reading research demonstrate the power of new spectra of research findings and methodologies to account for the cognitive activities entailed in school learning. And because, in the schools and classrooms across the country, reading is an essential tool for success, we can hope for significant advances in academic achievement as the policies and practices outlined in these pages become more widespread. (Anderson et al., 1984, p. viii)

The Commission on Reading concluded that phonics instruction should hold an important place in beginning reading instruction and recommended that "teachers of beginning reading should present well-designed phonics instruction" (Anderson et al., 1984, p. 118).

In work supported by the U.S. Department of Education Cooperative Agreement with the Reading Research and Education Center of the University of Illinois at Urbana-Champaign, Marilyn J. Adams's work *Beginning to Read: Thinking and Learning About Print* has extended our understanding and knowledge on the issue of phonics and its role in learning to read. After an exhaustive review of pertinent basic and applied research, Adams (1990) concludes,

> In summary, deep and thorough knowledge of letters, spelling patterns, and words, and of the phonological translations of all three, are of inescapable importance to both skillful reading and its acquisition. By extension, instruction designed to develop children's sensitivity to spellings and their relations to pronunciations should be of paramount importance in the development of reading skills. This is, of course, precisely what is intended of good phonic instruction. (p. 416)

More recently, the National Reading Council's *Preventing Reading Difficulties in Young Children* (Snow, Burns, & Griffin, 1998) and the National Reading Panel's (NRP's) *Teaching Children to Read: An Evidence-Based Assessment of the Scientific Research Literature on Reading and Its Implications for Reading Instruction* (National Institute of Child Health and Human Development, 2000a) provide further support for the importance of phonics in reading instruction. The NRP examined the research literature and concluded that "the meta-analysis revealed that systematic phonics instruction produces significant benefits for students in kindergarten through 6th grade and for children having difficulty learning to read" (p. 9).

Hence, the question regarding phonics instruction no longer appears to be whether it should be included in beginning instruction. Instead, the essential question is one of determining how phonics can be taught most effectively (Manning, 2004; McCardle & Chhabra, 2004; Moats, 2007; Spear-Swerling, 2007).

To assist teachers in teaching phonics effectively, several basic principles should underlie their actions:

1. Phonics must be viewed as a means to an end, not an end in itself. The purpose of phonics is to assist children in systematically decoding words that are unknown to them by teaching them the relationships that exist between letters and speech sounds.

2. Phonics will not work for all children. As with other methods of teaching reading, its effectiveness will run the gamut from ineffective to extremely effective. A challenge for teachers is to determine the proper match between phonics and the individual child and his or her learning style. This includes appropriate teaching responses to the changing demographics of diverse languages and cultural expectations that are now found in classrooms in the United States (Branum-Martin & Foorman, 2010; Byrd, 2008; Chen, 2009; Francis & Mehta, 2010; Genishi & Haas Dyson, 2009; Lane et al., 2009).

3. Phonics helps only if the unknown word is part of the reader's speaking–listening vocabulary. Since English language learners may not receive the necessary scaffolding for new vocabulary in their home, it is essential to encourage all parents and other caregivers, including teachers, to read aloud daily to beginning readers and provide them with guidance in learning not only the pronunciation of new words but their multiple meanings as well (Fan, 2003; Wallace, 2007). Learning new vocabulary and multiple definitions for new high-utility words is of particular importance in addressing the needs of English language learners whose performance on national assessments continues to be a concern (Carlo et al., 2004). Teachers should pay close attention to the context in which unknown words are found and explain them in terms the learner understands. Take, for instance, the sentence "The boy ran to the sliet." Although you can venture a guess about the proper pronunciation of *sliet*, you have no way of knowing whether you are correct because it is a nonsense word and not part of your speaking–listening vocabulary. This process is doubly difficult for English language learners who may not be certain as to whether *sliet* is a legitimate English word (Adamson, 2006; Cox & Boyd-Batstone, 2009).

4. Phonics is a skill that must be used in conjunction with the skills of contextual and structural analysis. Smith (1982) identifies the relationship between phonics and context:

   > Phonic strategies cannot be expected to eliminate all the uncertainty when the reader has no idea what the word might be. But if the reader can reduce alternatives in advance—by making use of non-visual information related both to reading and to the subject matter of the text—then phonics can be made most efficient. One way to reduce uncertainty in advance is to employ the mediating technique of making use of context. (p. 147)

5. In learning phonics, children must have the opportunity to see, hear, and say the components they are asked to learn. Initial instruction and practice

in phonics should, therefore, concentrate on oral activities (Jarmulowicz, 2006; Saxton, 2010). To accomplish this goal, teachers need to model continually the correct sounds of letters and words, and children need numerous opportunities to say these sounds and words. It is also important that teachers adhere to a standard of pronunciation that makes learning the sounds of the language consistent, avoiding dialectical markers that might inhibit student learning. Too many teaching materials require students to learn and/or practice phonics in a silent—and therefore ineffective—manner through the use of workbooks and other paper-and-pencil activities.

6. Phonics can be taught by using synthetic (explicit) and/or analytic (implicit) approaches to instruction. Although it must be understood that there is more than one significant difference between the synthetic and analytic approaches to phonics, the most basic difference between the two should be noted. Synthetic programs generally emphasize learning individual sounds, often in isolation, and follow with instruction that teaches children how to blend these individual sounds to form words (a part-to-whole approach). For instance, in the word *bat*, children would first sound out the isolated sounds (/b/ buh, / ă/ ah, /t/ tuh) and then blend them together to pronounce *bat*. Analytic programs, on the other hand, begin with whole words and identify individual sounds as part of those words. Teaching reading by starting with a whole word is a top-down approach because frequently the focus of instruction is on the meaning of the word, not on its constituent sounds. Efforts are made to avoid pronouncing letter sounds in isolation (a whole-to-part approach). On this point, the Commission on Reading (Anderson et al., 1984) writes,

> In the judgment of the Commission, isolating the sounds associated with most letters and teaching children to blend the sounds of letters together to try to identify words are useful instructional strategies. These are the strategies of explicit phonics. However, research provides insufficient justification for strict adherence to either overall philosophy. Probably, the best strategy would draw from both approaches. (p. 42)

In *Beginning to Read: Thinking and Learning About Print—A Summary*, Stahl, Osborn, and Lehr (1990) recommend the use of explicit instruction in phonics:

> Because most phonemes cannot be pronounced without a vowel, many programs avoid or limit the use of isolated phonemes in their instruction. This practice often leads to potentially confusing instruction. The advantages of asking students to articulate phonemes in isolation outweigh the disadvantages. . . . Phonemes are the basic sounds that make up words in a language. Because beginning readers frequently have difficulty analyzing the sound structures of words, reading programs should include explicit instruction in blending. (p. 126)

The previously cited NRP report (National Institute of Child Health and Human Development, 2000a) further supports the inclusion of systematic synthetic phonics instruction:

> Systematic synthetic phonics instruction had a positive and significant effect on disabled readers' reading skills. These children improved

substantially in their ability to read words and showed significant, albeit small, gains in their ability to process text as a result of systematic synthetic phonics instruction. This type of phonics instruction benefits both students with learning disabilities and low-achieving students who are not disabled. Moreover, systematic synthetic phonics instruction was significantly more effective in improving low socioeconomic status (SES) children's alphabetic knowledge and word reading skills than instructional approaches that were less focused on these initial reading skills. (p. 9)

7. "Phonics instruction should be kept simple and it should be completed by the end of second grade for most children" (Anderson et al., 1984, p. 118).

Through improved instruction, gains in reading achievement will be realized. Yet it has become painfully clear that too many teachers received inadequate emphasis on phonics in preservice course work and lack basic knowledge that would allow them to present well-conceived and effective phonics instruction and be confident of its outcome for the learner (Barnyak & Paquette, 2010; Byrd, 2008; Cunningham, Stanovich, & Stanovich, 2004; Honawar, 2009; Joshi, 2009a, 2009b; MacDonald Connor, Son, Hindman, & Morrison, 2005; Podhajski, Mather, Nathan, & Sammons, 2009; Pufpaff, 2010; Spear-Swerling, Brucker, & Alfano, 2006).

The following chapters are designed to overcome this limiting factor by providing prospective teachers with a phonics knowledge base and teaching strategies that support it. Both will help teachers provide beginning readers with programs based on well-established principles of effective reading instruction.

CHAPTER 1: PRACTICE

1. Phonics (is, is not) the single most important factor in reading success. (Circle one.)

2. For most children, phonics instruction should be completed by the end of _____ grade.

3. Phonics is most effective when it is utilized with skills such as _____ and _____ analysis.

4. The purpose of phonics is to assist children in systematically decoding words that are unknown to them by teaching them the relationships that exist between _____ and _____.

5. Phonics programs that emphasize the learning of individual sounds, often in isolation, and follow with instruction that teaches children how to blend these individual sounds to form words are known as (analytic, synthetic) programs. (Circle one.)

6. (Analytic, Synthetic) phonics programs begin with whole words and identify individual sounds as parts of those words. (Circle one.)

7. Explain the importance of learning high-utility vocabulary words for English language learners:

   _____

   _____

   _____

   _____

8. Think back to your earliest school experiences. Visualize the methods by which you were taught to read. What role did phonics play?

   _____

   _____

   _____

   _____

9. Why is it instructionally ineffective to have children practice phonics by filling out workbook pages and ditto sheets?

   _____

   _____

   _____

   _____

   _____

   _____

10. Explain the following statement: "Phonics must be viewed as a means to an end, not an end in itself."

   _____

   _____

   _____

   _____

   _____

   _____

   _____

11. Summarize the latest research as it relates to the use of systematic synthetic phonics instruction in beginning reading programs.

_____

_____

_____

_____

_____

_____

_____

POINTS TO PONDER: AN INVITATION TO DIALOGUE

With a partner or with a small group of other educators, discuss the following questions:

12. What is the hardest aspect of teaching phonics for you?

13. When teaching phonics, which aspects do children in your classroom find most challenging?

14. What are some of the effective resources offered by the required reading material within your classroom?

15. How do you integrate meaningful language into your phonics lessons?

For pronunciation standards and additional information regarding definitions used in this text, readers are encouraged to consult _Merriam-Webster's Online Dictionary_ at http://www.m-w.com.

2 Phonics Pretest

This pretest is designed to provide readers with feedback that should assist them in assessing their knowledge of phonics content. An analysis of results will help identify specific content problems and provide a focus as readers work through the text. Each question is coded for easy reference to the text location where additional information related to the content is found. Where itemized lists are cited, the page number and then the list number are cited. For example, "40.20" indicates the information is found on page 40 at list item number 20.

MATCHING

Match the words listed below with the appropriate definitions numbered 1 to 10.

a. phoneme	f. grapheme
b. digraph	g. macron
c. syllable	h. closed syllable
d. phonogram	i. consonant blend
e. phonics	j. diphthong

_____ 1. Two letters that stand for a single phoneme.

_____ 2. A letter or combination of letters that represents a phoneme.

_____ 3. Any syllable that ends with a consonant phoneme.

_____ 4. A method in which basic phonetics, the study of human speech sounds, is used to teach beginning reading.

_____ 5. The smallest *sound* unit of a language that distinguishes one word from another.

_____ 6. A letter sequence comprised of a vowel grapheme and an ending consonant grapheme(s).

_____ 7. A *single vowel sound* made up of a blend of two vowel sounds in immediate sequence and pronounced in one syllable.

_____ 8. Sounds in a syllable represented by two or more letters that are blended together without losing their own identities.

_____ 9. A unit of pronunciation that consists of a vowel alone or a vowel with one or more consonants.

_____ 10. The symbol placed over a vowel letter to show it is pronounced as a long sound.

TRUE–FALSE

_____ 11. The irregularity of vowel sounds is a basic problem of phonics.

_____ 12. The *schwa* sound is generally spelled in a consistent manner.

_____ 13. Phonics is the most important skill required for effective reading.

_____ 14. Synthetic phonics teaches students explicitly to convert letters into sounds and then blend the sounds to form recognizable words.

_____ 15. A grapheme may be composed of one or more letters.

_____ 16. Each syllable must contain only one vowel letter.

_____ 17. In decoding multisyllabic words, syllabication should precede the application of vowel generalizations.

_____ 18. There are approximately 100 ways to spell the 44 phonemes.

_____ 19. By the time the average child enters school, his or her auditory discrimination skills are fully developed.

_____ 20. The history of phonics shows that a phonics approach to teaching reading has been looked on favorably by most reading authorities over the past 50 years.

_____ 21. Bilingual children learning English benefit from highly explicit phonics instruction.

_____ 22. Changing demographics in the United States makes it highly likely that more than one language will be spoken in your classroom.

_____ 23. Changes in technology are significantly changing instruction in phonics.

_____ 24. Bilingual children in English-speaking classrooms typically progress at the same level as their peers.

_____ 25. Dialogue versus monologue is an effective teaching strategy when working with children learning phonics.

MULTIPLE CHOICE

_____ 26. Which of the following is a sound?
   a. grapheme
   b. vowel
   c. digraph
   d. none of the above

_____ 27. Which of the following words contains an open syllable?
   a. love
   b. son
   c. through
   d. fire

_____ 28. Which of the following words contains a digraph?
   a. fly
   b. bring
   c. blond
   d. home

_____ 29. Which of the following words contains letters that represent a diphthong?
   a. low
   b. meat
   c. through
   d. boy

_____ 30. How many phonemes are represented by the word _night_?
   a. 1
   b. 2
   c. 3
   d. 5

_____ 31. How many phonemes are represented by the word _boat_?
   a. 1
   b. 2
   c. 3
   d. 4

_____ 32. Which of the following pairs contains the same vowel phoneme?
   a. book—room
   b. too—shoe
   c. wool—food
   d. none of the above

_____ 33. Which of the following letters do not represent phonemes that are identified by their own name?
   a. t and s
   b. b and d
   c. y and z
   d. c and q

_____ 34. Which of the following consonant letters are most phonemically inconsistent in representing more than one sound?
   a. b and d
   b. c and s
   c. r and t
   d. m and p

_____ 35. Which of the following letter pairs represents a consonant blend?

    a. ch
    b. br
    c. th
    d. -ng

_____ 36. Which of the following nonsense words would most likely represent the "soft c" sound?

    a. cint
    b. cule
    c. coble
    d. calope

_____ 37. Which of the following nonsense words would most likely represent the "hard g" sound?

    a. giltion
    b. seg
    c. buge
    d. gymp

_____ 38. Which of the following consonant letters affects the vowel that precedes it?

    a. m
    b. t
    c. r
    d. none of the above

_____ 39. Which of the following words does not contain a consonant blend?

    a. fruit
    b. why
    c. blue
    d. flower

_____ 40. Which of the following words contains a closed syllable?

    a. low
    b. doubt
    c. dough
    d. boy

Circle the item in each list below that does not belong. Explain your reason for each.

41. sl   tr   bl   th   cl

_____

_____

_____

42. sh   wh   st   ng   ch

_____

_____

_____

43. a   y   i   s   w

_____

_____

_____

44. owl   out   low   pound

_____

_____

_____

45. gym   gum   game   goat

_____

_____

_____

The following questions should be answered by using the vowel generalizations that are often taught in elementary schools. Each question requires the vowel pronunciation contained in a nonsense word.

_____ 46. The *a* in *kaic* has the same sound as that found in:
    a. art.
    b. may.
    c. map.
    d. None of the above.

_____ 47. The *e* in *clek* has the same sound as that found in:
    a. be.
    b. err.
    c. end.
    d. None of the above.

_____ 48. The *o* in *kote* has the same sound as that found in:
    a. not.
    b. or.
    c. go.
    d. boy.

_____ 49. The *a* in *psa* has the same sound as that found in:
    a. art.
    b. may.
    c. map.
    d. None of the above.

_____ 50. The *i* in *sirp* has the same sound as that found in:

   a. in.
   b. girl.
   c. high.
   d. None of the above.

_____ 51. The *a* in *woab* has the same sound as that found in:

   a. art.
   b. may.
   c. map.
   d. None of the above.

_____ 52. The *u* in *kupp* has the same sound as that found in:

   a. hurt.
   b. up.
   c. rude.
   d. None of the above.

_____ 53. The *u* in *nue* has the same sound as that found in:

   a. hurt.
   b. up.
   c. use.
   d. None of the above.

Indicate where the syllabic divisions occur in the following vowel–consonant letter patterns, nonsense words, or real words. Knowledge of syllabication generalizations is essential. There are no consonant digraphs in questions 49 through 52 (C = consonant letter, V = vowel letter).

_____ 54. CVCVCC

   a. CVC-VCC
   b. CV-CVCC
   c. CVCV-CC
   d. CV-CV-CC

_____ 55. CVCCVC

   a. CV-CCVC
   b. CVCC-VC
   c. CVC-CVC
   d. CV-CC-VC

_____ 56. CVCCV

   a. CVC-CV
   b. CV-CCV
   c. CVCC-V
   d. C-V-CCV

_____ 57. CCVCVCC

     a. CCVC-VCC
     b. CCV-C-VCC
     c. CC-VC-VCC
     d. CCV-CVCC

_____ 58. intayed

     a. in-tay-ed
     b. in-tayed
     c. in-ta-yed
     d. intay-ed

_____ 59. makution

     a. ma-ku-tion
     b. mak-u-tion
     c. mak-u-ti-on
     d. ma-ku-ti-on

_____ 60. sleble

     a. sleb-le
     b. sleble
     c. sl-e-ble
     d. sle-ble

_____ 61. exanthema

     a. exan-the-ma
     b. ex-an-the-ma
     c. ex-an-them-a
     d. e-xan-the-ma

_____ 62. getker

     a. ge-tker
     b. get-ker
     c. getk-er
     d. getker

Reading programs often introduce long and short vowel sounds based on spelling patterns. In the following patterns (V = vowel letter; C = consonant letter), indicate which vowel sound you would expect the pattern to represent (L = long sound; S = short sound).

_____ 63. VC

_____ 64. VCe (_e_ = final _e_ in word)

_____ 65. CVCC

_____ 66. CV

67. List three key roles teachers should play while teaching phonics in the multilingual classroom:

    a.

    b.

    c.

68. When diagnosing phonics ability in the classroom, why is it important to consider the cultural background of the learner?

_____

_____

69. How does the process of teacher self-reflection relate to phonics instruction?

_____

_____

_____

70. What evidence is there to support the notion that teacher preparation in phonics instruction at the preservice level needs to be augmented?

_____

_____

_____

_____

_____

_____

CHAPTER 2: PRACTICE

Check your answers against those listed in Appendix A. If you had difficulty, don't be discouraged. Rather, analyze your results to identify areas that gave you the most trouble. List these problem areas below. As you work through the text, use this information to provide a focus for your study.

_____

_____

_____

_____

_____

_____

CUMULATIVE REVIEW: CHAPTERS 1 AND 2

1. The major word-recognition methods include phonics, whole-word methodology, _____, _____, _____, _____, and dictionary use.

2. Generally, the phonics instruction that appeared 35 years ago (is, is not) the same as that taught today. (Circle one.)

3. There (are, are not) significant research data that show the importance of phonics in beginning reading instruction. (Circle one.)

4. According to the latest research, the advantages of systematic synthetic phonics instruction (outweigh, do not outweigh) the disadvantages. (Circle one.)

5. Over the past 50 years, using a phonics approach to teaching beginning reading (has, has not) been consistently looked on favorably by most reading authorities. (Circle one.)

6. Learning letter sounds in isolation and blending them together to form words is an example of (synthetic, analytic) phonics. (Circle one.)

7. Why do most authorities suggest that phonics instruction be completed by the end of second grade for most children?

   _____

   _____

   _____

   _____

   _____

   _____

8. Explain the difference between explicit (synthetic) phonics instruction and implicit (analytic) phonics instruction.

   _____

   _____

   _____

   _____

   _____

9. From what you know about the whole-language philosophy, do you believe it is compatible with the teaching of phonics? Explain.

_____

_____

_____

_____

_____

_____

10. If an unknown word is not part of a reader's speaking–listening vocabulary, why will phonics be of little value in the process of decoding?

_____

_____

_____

_____

_____

3 Phonics Vocabulary and Phonemes

VOCABULARY

Although a more detailed glossary appears at the end of this text (see the Glossary on page 129), an introduction to pertinent vocabulary at this juncture will assist readers of this text. Ultimately, the following vocabulary words should be learned to the point where all meanings are understood instantly (a state known as *automaticity*). Related terms are grouped together.

phonics: A method in which basic phonetics, the study of human speech sounds, is used to teach beginning reading. Teachers teach phonics, not phonetics.

phonetics: The study of human speech sounds.

phoneme: The smallest *sound* unit of a language that distinguishes one word from another. Examples: the phoneme /h/ distinguishes *hat* from *at*; the words *tell* and *yell* are distinguished by their initial phonemes /t/ and /y/. This text indicates that there are 44 phonemes in the American-English language. This number varies, however, according to different authorities and/or dialects. Slash marks, //, are used throughout the text to indicate that the reference is to a *sound* and not a *letter*.

phonemic awareness: The ability to recognize spoken words as a sequence of individual sounds. Being able to distinguish or differentiate between the sounds that make up a word and apply this knowledge as it relates to the written form of a word is an essential skill in beginning reading (Jongejan, Verhoeven, & Siegel, 2007; Beard et al., 2009). Phonemic awareness is not phonics, but rather an important step toward phonics knowledge. Second language learners (L2s) who already possess knowledge of an alphabetic system frequently apply this knowledge to learning the second language (Branum-Martin, 2006; Domyei, 2009; Gabriele, Troseth, Martohardjono, & Otheguy, 2009; Grinstead, 2009).

consonant: A sound represented by any letter of the English alphabet except *a, e, i, o, u, w, y.* Consonants are sounds made by closing or restricting the breath channel.

consonant blend: Sounds in a syllable represented by two or more letters that are blended together without losing their own identities. Examples: *blue* /b/ /l/; *gray* /g/ /r/; *brown* /b/ /r/; *twig* /t/ /w/; *street* /s/ /t/ /r/; *flip* /f/ /l/.

vowel: A sound represented by *a, e, i, o, u* and sometimes *y* and *w* in the English alphabet. Vowels are sounds made without closing or restricting the breath channel. Saying the names of the vowels out loud will cause the vocal cords to vibrate. This characteristic of sounds is called *voicing* and helps beginning readers to hear distinctions between sounds. Vowels that record their long sounds when said aloud are always voiced. It is important to understand that speech sounds are categorized by where they are produced in the vocal system. The tongue, palate, uvula (the little flap of tissue at the rear of the mouth), and teeth all influence the way sounds are produced. As you will see later, the place of articulation within the vocal mechanism determines how speech sounds are coded by the use of various pronunciation guides called *diacritical marks*. Dictionaries standardize these pronunciations by providing pronunciation guides. Linguists categorize speech sounds according to where they are produced within the vocal mechanism.

diphthong: A single vowel sound made up of a glide from one vowel sound to another in immediate sequence and pronounced in one syllable. Examples: /oi/ in *oil* and b*oy*, /ou/ in h*ou*se, /ow/ in *owl*, and /ew/ in *few*. (Phonetics would consider that some single-letter vowels represent diphthongs. For the purposes of teaching reading, however, only /oi/ and /ou/ will be considered diphthongs.)

r-controlled vowel: When a vowel letter is followed by the letter *r*, it affects the vowel sound so that it is neither short nor long. For example, in *her*, the vowel sound becomes /û/; in *dare*, it becomes /â/; in *for*, it becomes /ô/; in *car*, it becomes /ä/.

schwa sound: An unstressed sound commonly occurring in unstressed syllables. It is represented by the symbol /ə/ and closely resembles the short sound for *u*. Examples: *a* in *about*; *o* in *occur*; *i* in *pencil*; *u* in *circus*. The schwa sound is the most common vowel sound in English and may be represented by any of the vowel letters.

grapheme: A letter or combination of letters that represents a phoneme (sound). Examples: the phoneme /b/ in *bat* is represented by the grapheme *b*; the phoneme /f/ in *phone* is represented by the grapheme *ph*. There are more than 200 ways to spell the phonemes. For example, /f/ can take the form of *f* in *fine*, *gh* in *cough*, and *ph* in *elephant*. This is an example of three different graphemes representing the same phoneme.

digraph: Two letters that stand for a single phoneme (sound). Examples: *th*in /th/; *each* / ē /; *shop* /sh/; b*oy* /oi/; l*ook* /o͝o/; ra*ng* /ng/; f*ew* /oo/. A digraph is simply a grapheme of two letters, but it is important to note that it may be represented by a combination of either two vowels or two consonants. Sometimes the letter combination "æ" is also referred to as "The Digraph" and is a special symbol used in the International Phonetic Alphabet.

onset: The consonant sound(s) of a syllable that come(s) before the vowel sound. (Examples are included with the definition of *rime* below.)

rime: The part of a syllable that includes the vowel sound and any consonant sound(s) that come(s) after it. The graphic representation of a rime is referred to as a *phonogram*. Following are examples of both onsets and rimes.

Word	Onset	Rime	Phonogram
mat	/m/	/at/	at
pig	/p/	/ig/	ig
at	—	/at/	at
split	/spl/	/it/	it

phonogram: A letter sequence comprised of a vowel grapheme and (an) ending consonant grapheme(s), such as *-ig* in *wig, dig, big* or the *-ack* in *back, tack, sack*. From phonograms, we can generate word families.

syllable: A unit of pronunciation consisting of a vowel alone or a vowel with one or more consonants. There can be only one vowel phoneme (sound) in each syllable. The syllable is considered to be the basic unit of pronunciation in English. Its processing for L2 learners has a direct effect on their comprehension of English (Mattys & Melhorn, 2005; Rogers & Lopez, 2008).

closed syllable: Any syllable that ends with a consonant phoneme (sound). Examples: come /m/; paste /t/; love /v/; ran /n/.

open syllable: Any syllable that ends with a vowel sound (phoneme). Examples: see / ē /; may /ā/; boy /oi/; auto /ō/.

breve: The orthographic symbol (˘) placed over a vowel letter to show it is pronounced as a short sound (sometimes called an unglided vowel).

circumflex: The orthographic symbol (^) placed above vowel graphemes to indicate pronunciation.

macron: The orthographic symbol (‾) placed over a vowel letter to show it is pronounced as a long sound (sometimes called a glided vowel).

umlaut: The orthographic symbol (¨) placed above vowel graphemes to indicate pronunciation.

It is useful for teachers to know how to insert English diacritical marks into their teaching materials when creating word processing documents. Please review this process in the section entitled Additional Web-Based Resources at the end of this text.

PHONEMES

As previously defined, phonemes are the smallest sound units of a language that distinguish one word from another. There are 44 phonemes in the English language; 25 of these are consonant phonemes, and 19 are vowel phonemes. The fact that there are more than 200 ways to spell the 44 phonemes creates confusion when learning how to read or spell in English. It is helpful to realize that English is not a static language. Many of the so-called irregular pronunciations that appear not to conform to phonics generalizations occur because they are used frequently, are borrowed or adapted from other languages with different pronunciation patterns, or have changed as a function of time. It is worthwhile for teachers to study exceptions to the rules or generalizations of phonics to discover information that will assist them in explaining the exceptions to beginning readers.

Consonant Phonemes—Pronunciation Key

Single Letters (18)
Each accompanying word represents the most common spelling of an initial consonant sound.

/b/	bat
/d/	did
/f/	fat
/g/	go
/h/	he
/j/	jam
/k/	come
/l/	let
/m/	me
/n/	no
/p/	pan
/r/	run
/s/	sat
/t/	ten
/v/	very
/w/	will
/y/	yes
/z/	zoo

Letters *c*, *q*, and *x* do not represent phonemes that are identified by their own names. Instead, these sound units are identified with like-sounding phonemes from the list above:

c represents the phonemes we associate with /s/ in *cent* or /k/ in *coat*.

q represents the phonemes we associate with /k/ /w/ in *quit* or /k/ in *antique*.

x represents the phonemes we associate with /g/ /z/ in *exit*, /k/ /s/ in *sox*, or /z/ in *xylophone*.

Double Letters (7)

/ch/	chair
/wh/	why
/ng/	song
/sh/	she
/th/	thin
/TH/	that
/zh/	measure

Vowel Phonemes—Pronunciation Key

Each accompanying word represents the most common spelling of vowel phonemes.

Long Vowels

/ā/	age
/ē/	ease
/ī/	ice
/ō/	old
/ū/	use

Short Vowels

/ă/	an
/ĕ/	end
/ĭ/	in
/ŏ/	odd
/ŭ/	up

Diphthongs

/oi/	oil, boy
/ou/	out, owl
/ew/	few

Double o

/o͞o/	too, rule
/o͝o/	good, pudding

Others

/ä/	father, star
/â/	dare, air
/û/	her, pearl
/ô/	auto, off, order

When vowel letters are followed by an *r*, they are known as *r-controlled.* This results in a sound that is neither short nor long.

Schwa /ə/: A schwa is a short, unstressed vowel that often occurs in unaccented syllables. The sound that schwa presents in a word varies depending on the vowel it represents and/or the sounds surrounding it.

a as in *about, senator*

o as in *occur, lemon*

e as in *effect, open*

i as in *pencil, notify*

u as in *circus, insulate*

au as in *authority*

ai as in *mountain*

ou as in *famous*

ea as in *pageant*

eo as in *dungeon*

oi as in *tortoise*

CHAPTER 3: PRACTICE

1. Circle each of the following terms that refers to a sound:

   phoneme   vowel   grapheme   rime

   diphthong   digraph   consonant   phonogram

2. Vowel sounds are usually represented by the following letters:

   _____, _____, _____,
   _____, and _____. Also,
   _____ and _____ sometimes represent
   vowels.

3. Circle each of the following words that contains an open syllable:

   son   go   dew

   love   through   fire

4. A(n) _____ is composed of two letters that stand for a single phoneme.

5. Underline any consonant digraph contained in the following words:

   blue   bring   the   street   shut   chill   train

6. Underline any vowel digraph contained in the following words:

   dew   look   love   soup   boy   go   beat

7. A(n) _____ is a special *single* vowel sound made up of a glide from one vowel to another. The phonemes that represent these sounds are /oi/ and /_____/.

8. Each syllable must contain one and only one vowel _____.

9. The orthographic symbol used to represent a long vowel sound is called a _____.

10. The orthographic symbol used to represent a short vowel sound is called a _____.

11. The letters that represent a diphthong are called a(n) _____.

12. A(n) _____ syllable ends with a consonant phoneme.

13. A special kind of grapheme that consists of two letters is called a(n) _____.

14. The study of human speech sounds is known as _____.

15. There are _____ phonemes in the English language, _____ consonant phonemes, and _____ vowel phonemes.

16. The schwa sound usually has a(n) (consistent, inconsistent) spelling. (Circle one.)

17. The inconsistent spelling of (consonant sounds, vowel sounds) is a basic problem of phonics. (Circle one.)

18. Check the pair(s) below that contain(s) the same vowel phoneme.

    a. book—room _____

    b. wool—food _____

    c. pool—stood _____

    d. too—shoes _____

19. Check each word below that contains a diphthong.

    a. coil _____

    b. out _____

    c. own _____

    d. owl _____

    e. could _____

20. The letters _____, _____, and
    _____ do not represent phonemes that are identified by
    their own names.

21. Fill in the proper consonant phoneme for each of the underlined letter(s).

center	/_____/	seizure	/_____/
chrome	/_____/	graph	/_____/
know	/_____/	germ	/_____/
sure	/_____/	whom	/_____/
wrong	/_____/	ghost	/_____/
white	/_____/	antique	/_____/

22. Fill in the proper vowel phoneme for each of the underlined letter(s).

paid	/_____/	turn	/_____/
die	/_____/	plaid	/_____/
boy	/_____/	owl	/_____/
eulogy	/_____/	pull	/_____/
wand	/_____/	said	/_____/
rule	/_____/	other	/_____/

23. How many phonemes are represented in the following words? Write each
    word using its phoneme pronunciation symbols.

sight	3	/s/ /ī/ /t/
sew	____	_____
sing	____	_____
blue	____	_____
ghost	____	_____
ship	____	_____
old	____	_____
boy	____	_____
bird	____	_____
both	____	_____

box   _____   _____

cent   _____   _____

comb   _____   _____

cow   _____   _____

low   _____   _____

24. Define the following phonics terms. If you are able to define them in your own words, you are well on your way to internalizing them and achieving automaticity.

Vowel:

_____

_____

_____

Grapheme:

_____

_____

_____

Phoneme:

_____

_____

_____

Consonant:

_____

_____

_____

Syllable:

_____

_____

_____

Macron:

_____

_____

_____

Open Syllable:

_____

_____

_____

Breve:

_____

_____

_____

Digraph:

_____

_____

_____

Rime:

_____

_____

_____

CUMULATIVE REVIEW: CHAPTERS 1 TO 3

1. There (are, are not) sufficient research data that show that systematic phonics instruction produces significant benefits for students learning to read.
   (Circle one.)

2. Systematic synthetic phonics instruction (has, does not have) a positive
   and significant effect on disabled readers' reading skills. (Circle one.)

3. Underline any letters in the following words that represent a consonant
   blend.

   that   she   blend   church   street   why   sing

4. Identify a word in which the letter _w_ functions as a vowel.

   _____

5. (Synthetic, Analytic) programs generally emphasize the learning of individual sounds, often in isolation, and follow with instruction that teaches
   children how to blend these individual sounds to form words. (Circle one.)

6. (Synthetic, Analytic) programs begin with whole words and identify individual sounds as part of those words. Efforts are made to avoid pronouncing letter sounds in isolation. (Circle one.)

7. What is the relationship between phonics and a person's speaking–listening vocabulary?

8. A (phonics, whole-word) emphasis would most likely be more effective with a word such as *pneumonia*. (Circle one.) Why?

9. What are the differences between a digraph and diphthong?

10. What is the difference between a consonant digraph and a consonant blend?

_____

_____

_____

_____

11. What is the difference between a phonogram and a rime?

_____

_____

_____

_____

_____

_____

_____

12. When the letter _r_ follows a vowel letter, how does it affect the vowel?

_____

_____

_____

_____

_____

_____

_____

13. How does knowledge of phonics foster independence in learning to read?

_____

_____

_____

_____

_____

_____

_____

14. The syllable in English (is, is not) the basic unit of pronunciation. (Circle one).

15. Second language learners who come from a language based on an alphabetic system are frequently able to apply knowledge of their first language

when learning a second. Why is this important when teaching them to read and write English?

_____

_____

_____

_____

_____

_____

POINTS TO PONDER: AN INVITATION TO DIALOGUE

The National Reading Panel's report (National Institute of Child Health and Human Development, 2000a) has had a tremendous influence on the development of reading materials for the schools. With another educator discuss the following:

16. How do the teaching materials used in your school's reading program define the core terms found in this chapter?

17. Which of the terms in this chapter and also in your school's reading material do you find the most difficult to understand? Which terms are the easiest to understand?

18. In your opinion, why is it important for teachers to know and understand diacritical marks used in reading instruction?

4 Emergent Literacy and Phonics

Although most attention to readiness factors has been placed in the context of formal education, the encounters children have with reading and writing before they begin school have become increasingly important in understanding how children learn to read. Sulzby and Teale (1991) explain emergent literacy as follows:

> Emergent literacy is concerned with the earliest phases of literacy development, the period between birth and the time when children read and write conventionally. The term *emergent literacy* signals a belief that, in a literate society, young children—even 1- and 2-year-olds—are in the process of becoming literate. This literacy is seen in not-yet-conventional behaviors; underlying the behaviors are understandings or hypotheses about literacy. Literacy learning is seen as taking place in home and community settings, in out-of-home care settings, and in school settings such as Head Start, pre-kindergarten, and kindergarten. (p. 728)

Thus, teachers can use the wide range of experiences children have had with language before formal school begins in assisting them to learn to read (Duursma, Romero-Contreras, Szuber, Proctor, & Snow, 2007; Francis & Mehta, 2010; Stuart, 1999). Children whose first language is other than English should be provided with an explicit, structured curriculum that allows them to practice a wide range of oral and visual skills (Ziegler, Granger, & Brysbaert, 2010). Children's understanding about print awareness, concepts of print, sense of story, oral language, and writing will have a significant bearing on their ultimate success in reading, writing, and spelling achievement (Grabner-Hagen, 2004; Heilmann, 2006; Verhoeven, 2000; Yesil-Dagli, 2011; Yovanoff, Duesbery, Alonzo, & Tindal, 2005).

Many factors have been identified as having some influence on success in beginning reading. Intelligence, general health, vision, hearing, motor coordination, gender, listening ability, language development, auditory discrimination, visual discrimination, background experience, emotional adjustment, story sense, age, phonemic awareness, and knowledge of letter names head the list of factors that have been discussed in methods texts over the past 35 years (Harris & Smith, 1986; Searfoss & Readence, 1994; Spache & Spache, 1986). For the purposes of this text, only those factors relating most directly to a phonics approach to reading are discussed at length.

ORAL LANGUAGE

Research has shown that a positive relationship exists between oral language and reading achievement (Beron, 2004; Blackman, 1984; Bowyer-Crane et al., 2008; Cutting, Cole, Levine, & Mahone, 2009; Edmiaston, 1984; German & Newman, 2007; Geva, 2006; Rosenthal, Baker, & Ginsburg, 1983). It appears that oral language serves as an essential foundation on which reading instruction can and should be built. Furthermore, the Russian psychologist Vygotsky (Flavell, 1977) believed that for young children to have thoughts, they must say them out loud. In essence, if Vygotsky was correct, to silence young children is to silence their thoughts. For this reason, teachers must understand the significance of oral language in beginning reading instruction and learning in general and include activities in the curriculum that build on the language skills children bring to school.

When it comes to oral language development in the classroom, all teachers should be mentors, translators, and guides for their students. Nowhere are these characteristics more critical than in the multilingual classroom. Reading mentors should take responsibility for the emotional and social welfare of their students. This takes the application of cultural knowledge and judgment related to the diverse learners and their particular backgrounds as they manifest themselves in the classroom. Considering the fact that today's classrooms reflect a wide diversity of cultural and linguistic backgrounds, another characteristic of an effective mentor is sensitivity toward these differences.

As a guide, the teacher's role might best be imagined as one where the teacher knows the linguistic territory of English and actively models this knowledge for her students. This can be a daunting task, especially when you consider that there may be multiple language bases other than English in any one classroom.

As a translator, the teacher models the learning of the structures of reading from phonemic awareness through the development of comprehension. Translation is especially important in the study and acquisition of vocabulary, both in its oral and in its written and morphological forms. Since morphology deals with the study of meanings, pointing out to L2 learners the cross-cultural and linguistic linkages between English and Latin-based languages such as Spanish and French, for example, helps to make significant transitions possible for students as they learn English. It is not unreasonable to expect that the best translators in this regard are those teachers who have facility in the native languages of their students. While it is unlikely that a teacher will know all the languages represented within a multilingual classroom, targeting the statistically most dominant or prevalent language represented by students becomes a matter of priority with far-reaching implications. Even a cursory examination of the field of bilingual education indicates an enormous growth in research related to addressing the needs of L2 learners since the last edition of this book. Since learners approach the acquisition of a second language in many complex and varied ways, it is important for teachers to understand the cognitive processes that lead to communicative competence. An excellent review of these processes may be found in

H. Douglas Brown's book, *Principles of Language Learning and Teaching* (2007). Additional helpful resources may be found in Coppola and Primas's *One Classroom, Many Learners: Best Literacy Practices for Today's Multicultural Classrooms* (2009).

Searfoss and Readence (1994) suggest that the rationale for oral language instruction should be based on three key processes:

1. Oral-language programs should utilize real experiences children have both in and out of school.

2. Oral-language development should be viewed as an integral part of the whole school day, planned but arising from naturally occurring events in the classroom.

3. Oral-language (speaking and listening) activities should lead naturally into using the tools of reading and writing. Activities designed to develop oral language should be integrated with reading and writing. (p. 63)

The following is a sampling of the kinds of classroom activities that can be used to accomplish effective oral language instruction.

Activity 1:   Read to children often. This activity has a positive effect on language development and can have an impact on children's attitudes toward reading. The physical context of the reading event should be warm, nurturing, and supportive. Since parents and caregivers are typically intimately aware of the child's interests and prior knowledge, their selection of developmentally appropriate reading material is crucial. Jim Trelease's (1995, 2006) book *The New Read-Aloud Handbook* is an excellent resource for both parents and educators in the identification and selection of books to be read aloud.

Activity 2:   Each day, provide children with numerous opportunities to express themselves. To accomplish this, set up situations that allow students to share experiences, ask questions, develop stories to be shared with others, resolve problems through language, and express attitudes and feelings. When teachers spend time at the beginning of the school day in activities such as Show and Tell or Bring and Brag, they provide children with appropriate opportunities to express themselves orally. Activities that promote oral language sharing also provide the teacher with opportunities to expand the vocabularies of their students and make sense of classroom activities and assignments for L2 learners. Recent research (Huang, Cunningham, & Finn, 2010) suggests that L2 learners benefit from oral activities in the classroom at multiple levels, including the development of reading comprehension elements related to main ideas and related detail. It is also clear that oral language activities strengthen the relationship between reading and writing for all children in the classroom, especially L2s (Restrepo, Castilla, Schwanenflugel, Neuharth-Pritchett, & Aroboleda, 2010; Spear-Swerling, 2007; Spear-Swerling & Brucker, 2006; Tam, Heward, & Heng, 2006).

Activity 3:   Use patterned books along with rhymes, poems, and songs to help develop children's oral language. Because these types of materials are very predictable, children can join quickly in the reading process (Hadaway, Vardell, & Young, 2001).

Activity 4:   Develop language-experience stories using the children's natural language. In this process, children use language to explore a common experience. Once this oral exploration is exhausted, the teacher tells the class she would like to write a story about their experiences. Using the children's own language, the teacher takes dictation and writes out their story on a large chart-paper tablet that is then used as reading material children can begin to read. This procedure helps children come to understand that what is said can be written down and preserved to be used later through the act of reading. Students frequently ask if it is appropriate to change the grammar of the child, or the group of children if the teacher is doing a whole-class experience story, as they dictate the story. It is important to remember that grammar is a reflection of the linguistic and cultural context from which the learner comes. Grammatical rules are arbitrary and a function of convention and standardization. This is also true of spelling. As the teacher functions as a transcriber in the creation of the experience story, filtering spelling is usually less problematic than changing syntax, or the order of the words the child or children present, and grammar. L2 learners bring varying degrees of linguistic competence related to their first language to the task of learning their second. Since the language experience story is dictated to the teacher, syntactic difference such as where nouns are modified (usually before the noun in English, but after the noun in French, for example) may cause meaning changes to the dictated story. It is good policy to seek the permission of those dictating a story before the teacher arbitrarily changes grammar. Keep in mind that changing what students dictate without explanation does little to teach children why their oral language was changed. Seeking permission and explaining why changes must occur within a meaningful dialog (Anderson, 2002; Wells, 2007) provides a golden opportunity for a teachable moment, especially for L2 learners (Brice, 2002; Gerber et al., 2004; McCardle & Hoff, 2006).

PHONEMIC AWARENESS

The high correlation that exists between the ability to recognize spoken words as a sequence of individual sounds and reading achievement has been well established over the past 35 years (Bradley & Bryant, 1983; Ehri, 1979; Golinkoff, 1978; Calfree, Lindamood, & Lindamood, 1973; Mann, 1994; Stuart, 1999; Tunmer & Nesdale, 1985). This correlation has generated interest in and research into the feasibility of teaching phonemic awareness to children at the kindergarten and first-grade levels. Lewkowicz (1980), in her analysis of 10 tasks that have been used by researchers or classroom teachers to test or teach phonemic awareness, came to the conclusion that two of these tasks, segmentation and blending, were basic and belonged in beginning instructional programs.

The reports of the Subgroups of the National Reading Panel *Teaching Children to Read* (National Institute of Child Health and Human Development, 2000b;

Strickland & Schickedanz, 2009) indicate that phonemic awareness can be taught and does help children learn to read and spell:

> Results of the meta-analysis showed that teaching phonemic awareness to children is clearly effective. It improves their ability to manipulate phonemes in speech. This skill transfers and helps them learn to read and spell. PA [phonemic awareness] training benefits not only word reading but also reading comprehension. PA training contributes to children's ability to read and spell for months, if not years, after training has ended. Effects of PA training are enhanced when children are taught how to apply PA skills to reading and writing tasks. (National Institute of Child Health and Human Development, 2000b, p. 2–40)

Teaching children to manipulate phonemes can be taught in a number of ways. Examples of activities appropriate at the readiness level (defined as kindergarten to first grade) follow:

Activity 1—Phoneme Isolation: Teach children to isolate sounds in words. This can be accomplished in several ways:

1. Teach children to hear and recognize initial sounds in words by prolonging or stretching pronunciation of initial sounds of words or iterating (repeating several times, especially the sounds recorded by vowels) the initial sounds of words.

2. Have children practice this skill by matching a sound with a picture of an object that represents that sound when read. For instance, say /b/ and have the children attempt to match it with a picture of a ball.

3. Have children practice identifying the initial sounds in words by reading words to them and asking them what sound each word starts with.

Activity 2—Phoneme Identity: Teach children to recognize common sounds in different words. For example, have them identify the sound that is the same in two words (*ball, boy*) and expand to three words (*ball, boy, bed*).

Activity 3—Phoneme Categorization: This activity requires children to recognize which word in a series of three or four words has a different sound (*ball, bed, cat*) (*ball, bed, boat, dog*).

Activity 4—Phoneme Counting: Ask children to count the number of sounds they hear as you read words slowly. Start with two-letter words and advance from there. Gradually reduce the slowness of pronunciation as children gain proficiency in this skill.

Activity 5—Phoneme Deletion: This activity requires children to identify a new word that is made when a phoneme is deleted from the original word. For example, they might be asked to say *sat* with the /s/ deleted. This activity may be more effective if the leftover words are also real words. Extending this activity to include ending and medial sounds should occur only after students become confident in their abilities to deal with beginning sounds.

Activity 6—Identification of Deleted Phonemes: This activity is similar to activity 5 because it relates to a deleted phoneme. In this activity, however, children are asked to identify the missing phoneme when comparing two similar sounding words. For instance, what sound do you hear in *mat* that is not in *at*?

Activity 7—Phoneme Substitution: Replace an identified sound with a new one and pronounce the new word. For instance, in the word *seat*, if you replace the /s/ with a /b/, how is the new word pronounced? (A similar activity is often used in which children are asked to identify new words through letter substitution rather than through sound substitution. It is suggested here that more work be done with sound substitutions.)

Activity 8—Phoneme Segmentation: Phoneme segmentation is the ability to isolate all the sounds of a word. Nation and Hulme (1997) found in their research that "phonemic segmentation is an excellent predictor of reading and spelling skill, even in the early stages of literacy development" (p. 166). Subsequent research corroborates this finding (Treiman, Bowey, & Bourassa, 2002). In teaching this skill, Lewkowicz (1980) found that it is extremely important for the teacher to prolong or stretch the word to be segmented and essential that the child attend to the articulatory clues, as well as the auditory clues, by slowly pronouncing the word.

1. Introduce children to the concept through modeling: Slowly say a word and emphasize its sounds; then identify each sound separately. For instance, read *dog* slowly and then identify /d/ /ô/ /g/ as the word's three sounds.

2. Provide practice for children by slowly reading words to them, emphasizing each sound. Ask children to articulate the individual sounds that make up each word. Start with two-letter words and advance from there to longer words as children become competent in voicing each sound in the words. At first, it is also effective to help students by identifying the number of sounds in each word. As students gain the ability to segment words, the number of sounds can be withheld.

Activity 9—Phoneme Blending: Blending is the process of recognizing isolated speech sounds and the ability to pronounce the word for which they stand when combined. The most appropriate time to "introduce blending seems likely to be when children have just 'gotten the hang of' segmentation and are practicing it intensively" (Lewkowicz, 1980, p. 697).

1. Have children practice blending two-phoneme words segmented into two parts (e.g., /n/ /ō/).

2. Have children practice blending three- or four-phoneme words segmented into two parts (e.g., /r/–/ă/ /t/; /s/ /t/–/ŏ/ /p/).

3. Advance to having children practice blending three- or four-phoneme words segmented into three parts (e.g., /d/–/ô/–/g/; /t/ /r/–/ĭ/–/p/).

Research seems to indicate, however, that focusing on one or two skills produces better results than focusing on many at the same time.

> Although all of the approaches exert a significant effect on reading, instruction that focuses on one or two skills produces greater transfer than a multi-skilled approach. Teaching students to segment and blend benefits reading more than a multi-skilled approach. Teaching students to manipulate phonemes with letters yields larger effects than teaching students without letters, not surprisingly because letters help children make the connection between phonemic awareness and its application to reading. Teaching children to blend the phonemes represented by letters is the equivalent of decoding instruction. Being explicit about the connection between phonemic awareness skills and reading also strengthens training effects. (National Institute of Child Health and Human Development, 2000b, pp. 2–41)

LETTER NAMES

To provide effective readiness instruction, teachers must understand the type of relationship that exists between knowledge of letter names and learning to read:

> A number of research studies have shown that letter knowledge is not necessarily a prerequisite for learning to read. On the other hand numerous studies have also shown that children who begin their schooling with knowledge of the ABC's are more likely to become better readers than children who lack this knowledge. For some time this was taken to mean that letter knowledge was helpful or necessary in learning to read. Most authorities now agree, however, that knowledge of the ABC's for entering school aged children is simply indicative of a host of factors that are often conducive to learning to read. Among these factors are a natural potential for learning to read, educational level of [the student's] parents, and [a] good reading environment at home. (Ekwall, 1976, p. 64)

Therefore, the readiness instruction in letter names for phonics must not be done under the false assumption that it will *cause* children to become good readers. Rather, it should be understood that children's knowledge of letter names will enable the teacher to communicate more effectively with them as instruction occurs.

VISION

Reading is a visual act that requires effective near-point (close) vision. Inadequate visual acuity may account for more than half of all reading failure (Shanker & Ekwall, 2003). Yet the types of tests often administered to children at the beginning stages of schooling simply measure far-point (distance) vision. Therefore, a cumulative file that contains information indicating that a child has successfully passed a vision test may be misleading. For this reason, teachers must be sensitive to signs in students that may indicate visual problems. Harris and Smith (1986) suggest that the following behaviors may be signs of visual problems:

- Cocking the head to read with only one eye.
- Holding the side of one's head when looking at the book or board.
- Rubbing eyes during reading.
- Having red and/or watery eyes.
- Holding the book too close to the face.
- Holding the book at arm's length.
- Complaining about headaches.
- Squinting or other indications of strain.
- Complaining about haziness or fading of printed symbols.

HEARING

Auditory acuity, the ability to hear sounds of varying pitch and loudness, is a critical factor in beginning reading. For instance, students who suffer hearing losses that affect their ability to hear high-frequency sounds may have difficulty in hearing certain consonants and consonant blends. Bond, Tinker, Wasson, and Wasson (1989) suggest that the following behaviors may be signs of auditory acuity problems:

- Inattention during listening activities.
- Frequent misunderstanding of oral directions or numerous requests for repetition of statements.
- Turning one ear toward the speaker or thrusting head forward when listening.
- Intent gaze at the speaker's face or strained posture while listening.
- Monotone speech, poor pronunciation, or indistinct articulation.
- Complaints of earache or hearing difficulty.
- Insistence on closeness to sound sources.
- Frequent colds, discharging ears, or difficult breathing.

If some of these behaviors are observed in students, they should serve as an alert that there may be a physical problem with either sight or vision that is hindering effective learning. If these behaviors continue after closer scrutiny, a referral should be made to an appropriate school official who has been trained to deal with these problems.

VISUAL DISCRIMINATION

Children develop their abilities to discriminate visually as they explore their environments through a combination of tactile and visual approaches. Spache and Spache (1986) point out that children who lack experiences with objects or forms at near-point range often have difficulty with reading.

Because reading is a visual act and requires visual discrimination ability, teachers should prepare children for phonics by providing exercises that help them discriminate between letters and words. Research results indicate that this task is best accomplished by having children practice using letters and words rather than pictures or various geometric shapes (Durkin, 1993).

Visual Discrimination Exercises

Visual discrimination exercises should progress in a logical sequence from simple to complex. Below are sequenced examples of exercises that can be used to further develop visual discrimination skills. Beyond these examples, teachers should be able to develop additional activities for improving visual discrimination.

Activity 1—Matching Letters: In this example, the student circles the letter on each line that is identical to the first letter of that line. (Examples progress from simple to complex.)

T	s	w	t	o
O	T	O	V	X
W	m	n	w	u
B	d	b	p	q

Activity 2—Matching Double Letters: In this example, the student circles the pair of letters on each line that is identical to the first two letters of that line. (Examples progress from simple to complex.)

Ok	Ts	xy	ok	mn
SP	OT	SP	MA	UW
Ab	Ap	ab	ba	pa
MN	NM	WN	MN	MW

Activity 3—Matching Words: In this example, the student circles the word on each line that is identical to the first word of that line. (Examples progress from simple to complex.)

big	Car	big	was	ran
TOP	CAR	SAW	TOP	BAG
boy	Big	bay	bag	boy
dog	God	dog	bog	dot

AUDITORY DISCRIMINATION

Children must be able to hear likenesses among and differences between sounds as they occur in spoken words. This ability or skill is known as *auditory discrimination*. A typical auditory discrimination test would ask children to recognize the fine differences between the phonemes used in English speech; this applies especially to L2 English learners (Navarra & Soto-Faraco, 2007). Hearing the differences between minimal pairs may not be just a matter of phonemic differences in hearing but also may include nonverbal cues associated with places of articulation such as the lips that help the learner to identify discrete differences between sounds. For instance, children might be asked to say whether word pairs that are read to them sound exactly the same or different. Minimal word pairs that differ by a single phoneme in the beginning position (hot—cot), middle position (met—mit), and ending position (sad—sat) are used with word pairs that are identical (man—man) to measure this skill. One study attempting to predict first-grade reading success based on tests of visual discrimination, auditory discrimination, and auditory vocabulary (Spache, Andres, Curtis, Rowland, & Fields, 1965) found that measures of auditory discrimination were the best overall predictors. These results suggest that auditory discrimination is a significant factor in beginning reading.

Measures of auditory discrimination provide only partial data when differentiating between children who need training and children who do not. In using auditory discrimination data, the following considerations should be kept in mind: Poor performance may, in fact, reflect a hearing loss rather than a lack of auditory discrimination, and some speech sounds are often not mastered by the age of 6 or 7 (Spache & Spache, 1986). These limitations, however, do not render auditory discrimination measures worthless. If the test results are used with limitations in mind and are complemented by other pertinent data such as teacher observations, the student's classroom achievement, and medical information, auditory discrimination measures can provide valuable input regarding a child's readiness to use phonics in learning to read.

Auditory Awareness Exercises

Since oral language serves as the foundation on which reading skills are built, teachers should provide children with numerous experiences in both listening and speech. Activities similar to those listed here will allow children to work with language in a productive way.

Activity 1:   Read to children daily. Nursery rhymes and rhyming books provide children with opportunities to experience similar sounds in a patterned manner.

Activity 2:   Storybook reading provides opportunities for listening, but they should also provide children with meaningful opportunities for using oral language.

Activity 3: Have children identify the sounds heard in the classroom and around the school.

Activity 4: Have children close their eyes. Ask them to identify the sounds of snapping fingers, a pencil sharpener, tearing paper, chalkboard writing, and so on.

Activity 5: Play recordings of common sounds and have children identify them.

Activity 6: Have children play a game in which they have to identify sounds made by a child who imitates a sound from a specific place, such as a farm, airport, highway, zoo, and so on.

Auditory Discrimination Exercises

To provide more direct opportunities to improve auditory discrimination skills, you can guide children to work with the sounds of the English language, not simply sounds in general, as was done while building auditory awareness in the preceding examples. In addition, it is important for children either to hear someone else voicing the sounds or to say the sounds themselves *out loud*. Too often, auditory discrimination activities require children to identify the sounds, as represented by pictures, silently as they make decisions about likenesses and differences rather than having them name the pictures out loud. Activities can be used to provide practice in beginning, middle, and ending sounds. The instructor should introduce beginning sounds first, followed by ending sounds and finally middle sounds. Although the following activities are designed to practice beginning-sound discrimination, they can be modified to include work on the endings and middles of words.

Activity 1: Read word pairs to the class (e.g., cot--hot; man--men; sin--pin). Ask if they begin with the same sound or a different sound. Always keep in mind that the language used to instruct must be understood by students. If, in this example, they do not know what "same" or "different" means, the strategy will have no value (Ota, Hartsuiker, & Haywood, 2010; Seef-Gabriel, 2003).

Activity 2: Have children listen to a series of words that begin with the same consonant sound. Ask children to identify other words that begin with the same sound.

Activity 3: Read a series of words to children (e.g., cat, come, cane, man), have the entire class repeat all the words together, and ask them to say the one that does not belong.

Activity 4: Provide beginning sounds for the children (e.g., /s/) and ask them to say words that begin with the same sounds.

Activity 5: Introduce children to rhyming words through the use of nursery rhymes and poetry.

CHAPTER 4: PRACTICE

1. Emergent literacy (is, is not) concerned with the earliest phases of literacy development, the period between birth and the time when children read and write conventionally. (Circle one.)

2. What is the relationship between oral language and reading achievement? How are deficits in oral language development especially problematic for L2 learners?

   _____

   _____

   _____

   _____

   _____

3. _____ is the ability to recognize spoken words as sequences of individual sounds.

4. Phoneme_____ is the ability to isolate all the sounds of a word.

5. Phoneme_____is the process of recognizing isolated speech sounds and the ability to pronounce words for which they stand when combined.

6. The chapter identifies several skills teachers can use to teach children to manipulate phonemes. What does research suggest about using a multi-skilled approach to teach children to manipulate phonemes?

   _____

   _____

   _____

   _____

   _____

7. Numerous studies have shown that children who begin their schooling with knowledge of the ABCs are more likely to become better readers than children who lack this knowledge. Does it then follow that teaching children their ABCs will produce better readers? Why?

   _____

   _____

   _____

   _____

8. Why might a school cumulative file that contains information indicating that a child has successfully passed a vision test be misleading?

_____

_____

_____

_____

_____

9. Having children practice visual discrimination for reading by using pictures and geometric shapes (is, is not) an effective procedure. (Circle one.)

10. What implications does the concept of emergent literacy hold for teachers of beginning reading? Are these implications similar or different for children who are learning English as a second language?

_____

_____

_____

_____

_____

_____

CUMULATIVE REVIEW: CHAPTERS 1 TO 4

1. A(n) _____ is a part of the syllable that includes the vowel sound and any consonant sound(s) that come(s) after it.

2. A *single vowel sound* made up of a glide from one vowel to another in immediate sequence and pronounced in one syllable is called A(n) _____.

3. A *phonogram* is the graphic representation of A(n) _____.

4. Any syllable that ends with a vowel phoneme is called a(n) _____ syllable.

5. The sounds represented by *bl* in *blue* are called A(n) _____ _____.

6. A(n) _____ is a soft vowel sound closely resembling the short sound of *u* that commonly occurs in unstressed syllables.

7. The _____ is a symbol placed over a vowel letter to show that it is pronounced as a short sound.

8. The phoneme /oi/ is an example of A(n) _____.

9. (True–False) All digraphs are graphemes.

10. (True–False) All graphemes are digraphs.

11. If a child enters kindergarten reading at the third-grade level, do you believe that she should go through the phonics curriculum as set up by the district? Why?

    _____

    _____

    _____

12. Definecr the following phonic terms.

    Phoneme:

    _____

    _____

    _____

    Grapheme:

    _____

    _____

    _____

    Digraph:

    _____

    _____

    _____

    Onset:

    _____

    _____

    _____

13. (Phonics, Phonetics) is the method used to teach beginning reading. (Circle one.)

14. A closed syllable ends with A(n) _____ _____.

15. A letter or combination of letters that represents a phoneme is called A(n) _____.

16. (True–False) Implicit approaches to teaching phonics have proven more effective than explicit approaches.

17. A(n) _____ is a unit of pronunciation that consists of a vowel alone or a vowel with one or more consonants.

18. An unstressed sound commonly occurring in unstressed syllables and very closely resembling the short u sound is A(n) _____.

19. Provide a word that contains each of the following:

    Vowel digraph _____

    Consonant digraph _____

    Diphthong _____

    Schwa _____

    Blend _____

    Open syllable _____

    Closed syllable _____

20. Underline any consonant or vowel digraph in the following words:

    stew   the   why   star   meet   shut   glove   good   sing   glut

21. Underline the digraphs in the following words that represent diphthongs:

    boy   could   owl   out   point   cow   boil   own   coin   town

22. Fill in the proper consonant phonemes for each of the underlined letter(s):

    care   /_____/   song   /_____/

    why   /_____/   phone   /_____/

    measure   /_____/   whom   /_____/

    sox   /_____/   /_____/   chemist   /_____/

    quit   /_____/   /_____/   gym   /_____/

23. Fill in the proper vowel phonemes for each of the underlined letter(s):

    dare   /_____/   order   /_____/

    father   /_____/   star   /_____/

    awful   /_____/   pearl   /_____/

    rule   /_____/   good   /_____/

    owl   /_____/   hurt   /_____/

24. How many phonemes are represented in the following words? Write each
    word using its phoneme pronunciation symbols:

plum	4	/p/ /l/ /ŭ/ /m/
off	___	_____
future	___	_____
naked	___	_____
true	___	_____
plume	___	_____
funny	___	_____
queen	___	_____
mix	___	_____
hare	___	_____

POINTS TO PONDER: AN INVITATION TO DIALOGUE

25. Linguists often discuss sounds that are "minimal pairs" or sounds that
    vary in small ways. Why is it important that teachers use careful articu-
    lation when working with children in phonics? Why do you think it is
    important to have children look at you when you are articulating words?

26. Research suggests that activities such as listening to music enhance the
    capacity of children to hear the difference between sounds in English
    (Chappell, 2008). How could you incorporate the use of music in your
    classroom?

27. Do you intentionally use gestures when you teach? If so, how does your
    use of gestures help children learn concepts such as phonemic segmenta-
    tion or phoneme blending?

5 Phonic Generalizations

Much has been written about the utility of phonic generalizations over the past 35 years. Although some work in the area had been accomplished before 1960, an article by Clymer (1996) questioning the appropriateness of the many phonic generalizations taught at the time gave rise to several research projects designed to examine and extend what Clymer studied.

In essence, Clymer analyzed the instructor's manuals of four widely used primary-grade readers and identified 121 generalizations: 50 vowel generalizations, 15 consonant generalizations, 28 ending generalizations, and 28 syllabication generalizations. Of these, 45 generalizations were selected arbitrarily for further study (each had to be specific enough to be applied to individual words). A list of 2,600 words was developed by combining the words introduced in the four readers with the words from the Gates Reading Vocabulary for the Primary Grades. Using *Webster's New Collegiate Dictionary* as the pronunciation authority, each applicable word was checked against the appropriate generalization. From this check, a "percent of utility" was computed for each generalization. For instance, if 10 words could be applied to a generalization, five of which followed the generalization and five of which did not, the generalization would have a 50% utility.

At the beginning of the study, Clymer postulated that a 75% utility was indicative of a useful generalization. Only 18 of the 45 generalizations satisfied this utility criterion (Clymer, 1963). The results of Clymer's study proved disturbing to him and others because they ran counter to what many instructors had been teaching for many years.

Clymer's research was followed by other studies on similar aspects of phonic generalizations. Bailey (1967) examined the 45 phonic generalizations studied previously by Clymer but extended the word list to include all words in the student textbooks from eight basal reading series, grades 1 through 6. She concluded that only six generalizations "were found to be simple to understand and apply, to be applicable to large numbers of words, and to have few exceptions" (p. 414). Emans (1967), using the same generalizations and procedures as Clymer, studied words beyond the primary level (grade 4) to determine the usefulness of phonic generalizations. He found that 16 of the 45 generalizations (Clymer's 5, 8, 16, 20, 22, 23, 24, 28, 30, 31, 32, 36, 38, 40, 41, and 45) met the criteria established by Clymer. Other studies (Burmeister, 1968; Caldwell, Roth, and Turner, 1978; Fuld, 1968; Gates; 1986, Hillerich, 1978; and Johnston, 2001) have addressed various aspects of phonic generalizations. Based on the results of those studies and an examination of current basal series, certain consonant and vowel generalizations stand out as having enough utility to be of value in phonics instruction (Johnston, 2001; Cunningham, 2004; Wernham, 2005; Boyer-Crane, 2008; Tindall , 2010; Cassady, 2010). Readers who wish to further investigate Clymer's work in regard to the usefulness of phonics generalizations, may find his research and resources relative to it readily available on the internet.

THE TEACHING CONTEXT OF THE PHONICS GENERALIZATIONS

Since the last edition of this text, significant changes in the assessment and delivery of phonics instruction have occurred in the United States. The advent of No Child Left Behind and the National Reading Panel's research and recommendations referred to elsewhere in this text, have had a profound influence on the nature of reading instruction. The concomitant sociological and linguistic changes that have occurred simultaneously to these national initiatives have also changed the face of America's classrooms. It is very likely that today's teacher will need to learn critical new skills in addressing the needs of both bilingual as well as bicultural learners in her classroom. Knowing, understanding, and applying the traditional phonics generalizations typically recommended in basal reading materials is simply not enough (Gallo, 2008; Manyak, 2008; Byrd, 2008; Brown, 2009). Today's teacher should also understand critical constraints to the learning of a primary language in relationship to a secondary language. Where earlier editions of this text were focused solely on the sound patterns mapped onto the graphic symbols used to represent them in English, now it is very important to know that children coming to the learning event may have very different linguistic and cultural determinants that significantly influence the way they learn to apply phonics in English (Hones, 2009; Chen, 2009). Following are recommendations which should assist the teacher in the effective application of phonics generalizations in the context of these linguistic and cultural changes in the classroom.

ACCURATELY HEARING SPEECH SOUNDS IS IMPORTANT

Clear, consistent articulation of speech sounds is important for all learners, but it is especially important to children learning English as a second language. Hadaway (2001) Rogers (2008), Geva (2006) suggest that the inability of the learner to properly hear targeted speech sounds because of random noise, poor articulation on the part of the teacher because of dialect, or because of insufficient volume, puts second language learners at a distinct disadvantage when compared to native language speakers. Second language learners have a greater need for clear signal processing in order to adequately develop their linguistic competence in the second language (Jarmulowicz, 2006). Because phoneme patterns of the bilingual's first or native language may be at odds with the phonemes used to articulate English speech, it is important that teachers model the distinctive feature differences between the phonemes of the respective languages (Seeff-Gabriel, 2003; Manyak, 2007). While this process is helpful for all learners, it is especially helpful to second language learners (Huang, 2010; Miller, 2006). Where a typically engaged classroom may generate constructive noise that would not normally disrupt learning, for the L2 learner, this noise may postpone the development of speech processing and severely interfere with the development of the capacity to hear the fine differences between speech sounds necessary to properly apply a generalization leading to accurate identification of a word (Strid, 2007). For some learning events, especially those related to the development of speech sounds used to articulate phonics generalizations, classrooms needs to be relatively quiet.

THE AGE WHEN SECOND LANGUAGE LEARNING OCCURS MATTERS

The age of the learner at the onset of second language learning is pivotal in the efficacy as well as the efficiency of the delivery of instruction (Stuart, 1999; Singleton, 2005). Reading instruction which seeks to broaden the linguistic competence of all learners in the classroom should be the goal of every teacher, but the timeliness of onset of language related instruction for the development of the linguistic competence of the bilingual learner is of particular importance (Jedynak, 2009; Menken, 2010). Regardless of the age old debate over the existence of a critical age for language learning, reading and language programs that strategically and deliberately plan and apply a synergy of language skills such as talking, reading and writing early in the learner's educational experiences appear to be more effective with young second language learners than those programs that start later. It is clear that language related intervention beginning as early as pre-school is more efficient in the delivery this synergy than those language intervention programs which are deferred until later in the educational process Birdsong (1999); Schmitt (2001); Rycik (2007); Roskos (2009). Delaying the delivery of language instruction for bilinguals has adverse negative, long ranging consequences to their learning (DeCapua, 2007; Yesil-Dagli, 2011).

LANGUAGE AND CULTURE ARE SIGNIFICANTLY INTERTWINED

To value a learner's language is to value their culture, and vice versa. Reading instruction should occur in the context of tolerance toward cultural and linguistic differences within the classroom. Learners need to be supported in the act of learning, and they should be shown that their prior knowledge and prior experiences are valued by the teacher. The learner should also be shown that this knowledge and experience has worth and contributes to the activities of the classroom in substantive and important ways. By valuing the language and the culture of the learner, the teacher is validating the learner herself. This is a powerful and potent motivator for further learning and helps to avoid the marginalization some children feel when their cultural or their language, or both, are characterized as substandard, having little or no bearing on what needs to be learned in the classroom (Thu, 2010). Children need frequent positive transactions with a teacher who esteems and values them for who they are. One manifestation of this esteem should be the overt valuing of the learner's language, its traditions, its history, and its application within the classroom (Genishi, 2009). Language and the identity of learners are inexorably connected. Because of this, teachers must exercise tolerance and acceptance at multiple levels, especially in regard to the linguistic and cultural heritages of the children in their classrooms (Huhtala, 2010).

CROSS-LANGUAGE TRANSFER

Using the primary language of the learner to assist in the process of reading instruction, yields better results than other methodologies which do not use the primary language as a tool of mediation. Teaching English by using the primary language of the learner encourages what is called cross-language effects, meaning that the structures of language, both within the L1 and within the L2, benefit from the study of language generally and this helps to more efficiently develop the communicative competence of the learner (Gabriele, 2009). When limitations to this effect do occur, it is likely that these are due to the limited application of resources, the context of the cultural norms in the learning environment, the socio-economic status of the learner and the context in which the learning takes place. Because these factors are so important to the ultimate success of the learner, teachers must be knowledgeable about the pedagogy of reading instruction as it applies to second language learning (Cunningham, 2004). In order to foster cross-language effects, teachers should directly identify and make meaningful, overt comparisons between elements of the primary language of the learner and the secondary language which in this case is English (Branum-Martin, 2010). Cross-language transfer is also aided by a constructive, cooperative relationship with the bilingual's home environment (Duursma, 2007).

PHONICS INSTRUCTION THAT WORKS

Systematic explicit instruction in phonics delivered by teachers well versed in reading curriculum is likely to have a more significant positive effect on learner outcomes, than those programs which are not systematic (Graves, 2005; Vaughn,

2006; Burke, 2009; Ota, 2010). Programs which focus on the foundational elements of reading, letter identification, phonological awareness, phonics, vocabulary and comprehension, are also more likely to yield positive results for learners than those programs which do not focus on these elements (Jongejan, 2007; Smith, 2008). When peer-mediated and peer assisted learning strategies (PALS) reading interventions are used by teachers in bilingual classrooms, positive effects on both native and non-native learners are significantly increased (Calhoon, 2007; McMaster, 2008). Effective reading instructional practices used with native English speakers are likely to be effective strategies to develop linguistic competence in non-native speakers (Tam, 2006). Sheltered instruction for at-risk bilingual children is effective (Graves, 2007; Malloy, 2007; Macaro, 2006). What do these instructional practices and procedures have in common that make them effective responses to teaching reading in a bilingual classroom? It should be clear that the preparation of the teacher is critical to the process of delivery of reading instruction. Is should also be clear that simply knowing the rules of the phonics generalizations in English is also not enough. It is necessary for teachers of reading to have a broad perspective on language as a whole, sensitive to, and knowledgeable about the array of languages represented in her classroom. While this task may seem daunting, it is important to remember that effective instruction in reading should benefit all students in the classroom regardless of their language base.

CONSONANT GENERALIZATIONS

Consonant generalizations are more consistent than vowel generalizations. The following appear to offer the most instructional value:

1. *c* usually represents the "soft c" as in *cent* and *race* when followed by the letters *e, i,* or *y*. Otherwise, the *c* usually represents the "hard c" as in *coat* and *cot*.

2. *g* usually represents the "soft g" as in *gym* and *wage* when followed by the letters *e, i,* and *y*. Otherwise, the *g* usually represents the "hard g" as in *go* and *nag*.

   When using these two generalizations, children should be taught that there are exceptions. If, when attempting to identify a word, they find that the generalization does not appear to work, children should be encouraged to try the other sound before seeking help.

3. The consonant digraph *ch* is usually pronounced /ch/ as in *church* but may also represent the sounds of /k/ as in *chemical* or /sh/ as in *machine*.

4. When identical consonant letters are next to each other, only one is usually heard as in *letter, call,* and *cannon*.

5. Certain consonant letters represent more than one sound. (See also items 1 and 2.)

	s		x
Smile	/s/	anxiety	/z/
Is	/z/	mix	/k/ /s/
Sure	/sh/	exit	/g/ /z/
pleasure	/zh/		

6. When a word ends in *ck*, it has the sound /k/ as in *book*.
7. When a word begins with *kn*, the *k* is silent as in *knit*.
8. When a word begins with *wr*, the *w* is silent as in *wrong*.
9. When a word begins with *gn*, the *g* is silent as in *gnat*.

VOWEL GENERALIZATIONS

Although the correspondence between vowel letters and sounds in English is less consistent than the correspondence between consonant letters and sounds, some consistency does exist and allows for the following vowel generalizations:

1. A single vowel letter in a syllable usually represents the short sound if it is not the final letter (cat, but, lot, met, mit).
2. A single vowel letter in a syllable usually represents the long sound if it is the final letter (he, hi, go, pa-per, ti-ger).
3. When two vowel letters in a syllable are separated by a consonant and one is a final *e*, the first usually records its long sound, and the *e* is silent (hope, late, cute).
4. When two successive vowel letters occur in a syllable and they are not any of the special digraphs (oi, oy, ow, ew, ou, oo, au), the first vowel letter is usually long and the second silent (especially ee—keep, ea—meat, ai—pain, ay—say, oa—load).

Because there are many exceptions to these generalizations, Spache and Spache (1986) recommend that children learn to use a systematic approach when meeting an unknown word. If the sound of the first letter or blend combined with context is not sufficient to "unlock" the word, a closer look at vowels is suggested. An application of appropriate vowel generalizations (see items 1 to 4) is used in the next attempt at correct pronunciation. If the vowel generalization fails, the other vowel sound should be attempted. Should these efforts fail, assistance from a dictionary or teacher would then be appropriate (Litt, 2007).

This systematic approach emphasizes that generalizations are only guidelines. When they do not work, other sounds should be attempted.

5. *ow* has two sounds, the /ō/ as in *own* and the /ou/ as in *cow*.

6. *oo* has two sounds, the /o͞o/ as in *food* and the /o͝o/ as in *foot*.

7. The *r* gives the vowel before it a sound that is neither long nor short.

8. The vowel digraphs *oi, oy, ou,* and *ow* blend into a single sound (diphthong) as in *boil, boy, out,* and *owl*.

9. *y* at the end of a word usually represents a vowel sound.

In teaching these generalizations, two approaches may be taken. One procedure would center on the teacher telling children about generalizations and having them apply those generalizations to specific words. This telling process is known as *deductive instruction*. For instance, a generalization like the following is taught first: "When there are two vowels side by side, the long sound of the first is heard, and the second is silent." Children are then asked to apply it to specific examples.

A second procedure would be described as *inductive instruction*. The inductive process begins with specifics and moves to generalizations about them. For instance, children might be asked to analyze the vowels in a group of words—boat, heat, rain, low—from which they will identify a common characteristic and ultimately develop a generalization to cover the pattern (in this example, first vowel long and second vowel silent).

Both approaches have their place in phonics instruction. For instance, inductive instruction provides children with opportunities for developing strategies of independent learning. On the other hand, deductive instruction has certain time advantages and can be used when efficient use of time becomes an important element in the teaching situation. In addition, not all children have success with the inductive approach. Consequently, a combination of the two processes can serve a valuable function in phonics instruction (Kerka, 2007; Tindall & Nisbet, 2010).

CHAPTER 5: PRACTICE

1. An analysis of Clymer's (1963) and more recent studies reveal that _____ generalizations generally have a greater utility value than do _____ generalizations.

2. Circle the following nonsense words in which *c* would most likely represent the "soft c" sound:

   cint   cule   cymp   sluce

3. The consonant digraph *ch* usually represents the phoneme / _____/. However, it may also represent the phonemes / _____/ and / _____/.

4. When identical consonant letters are next to each other, (both, only one) (are, is) usually heard. (Circle one of each.)

5. (Deductive, Inductive) teaching begins with specifics and moves to generalizations. It is analytic in nature. (Circle one.)

6. Circle the following nonsense words in which *g* would most likely represent the "hard g" sound:

      giltion   gultion   buge   seg

7. When a word begins with *kn*, the *k* is _____.

8. When the _____ _____ *ck* ends a word, it represents the phoneme /_____ /.

The following questions should be answered using the vowel generalization information presented earlier. Each question requires the vowel pronunciation contained in a nonsense word. Circle the correct answer.

9. The *e* in *slek* has the same sound as:

    a. *e* in *he.*

    b. *e* in *err.*

    c. *e* in *end.*

    d. *e* in *her.*

    e. None of the above.

10. The *a* in *swa* has the same sound as:

    a. *a* in *may.*

    b. *a* in *wand.*

    c. *a* in *add.*

    d. *a* in *art.*

    e. None of the above.

11. The *o* in *kote* has the same sound as:

    a. *o* in *cop.*

    b. *o* in *orange.*

    c. *o* in *go.*

    d. *o* in *out.*

    e. None of the above.

12. The *e* in *ceab* has the same sound as:

    a. *e* in *he.*

    b. e in *err.*

    c. e in *end.*

    d. e in *her.*

    e. None of the above.

13. The *o* in *woab* has the same sound as:

    a. *o* in *boy*.

    b. *o* in *go*.

    c. *o* in *out*.

    d. *o* in *cot*.

    e. None of the above.

14. The *u* in *knupe* has the same sound as:

    a. *u* in *up*.

    b. *u* in *run*.

    c. *u* in *hurt*.

    d. *u* in *use*.

    e. None of the above.

15. The *i* in *fif* has the same sound as:

    a. *i* in *high*.

    b. *i* in *girl*.

    c. *i* in *in*.

    d. *i* in *pine*.

    e. None of the above.

16. The *a* in *paic* has the same sound as:

    a. *a* in *art*.

    b. *a* in *name*.

    c. *a* in *map*.

    d. *a* in *swan*.

    e. None of the above.

17. A single vowel letter in a syllable usually represents the short sound if

    _____

    _____.

18. A single vowel letter in a syllable usually represents the long sound if

    _____

    _____.

19. When two vowel letters in a syllable are separated by a consonant and one is a final *e*, the first usually records its _____ sound, and the *e* is _____.

20. When two successive vowel letters occur in a syllable and they are not any of the special digraphs, the first usually records its _____ sound, and the second is _____.

CUMULATIVE REVIEW: CHAPTERS 1 TO 5

1. (True–False) It appears that a commitment to whole-word instruction is in direct opposition to using a phonics approach in any significant way.

2. The study of human speech sounds is called _____.

3. A _____ is the symbol used to represent a long vowel sound.

4. There is only one _____ phoneme in each syllable.

5. A phoneme is the _____ sound unit of a language that distinguishes one word from another.

6. The *oa* in *boat* is called a _____.

7. _____ _____ is the ability to hear likenesses and differences among sounds as they occur in spoken words.

8. Readiness to read (is, is not) something that exists in an absolute sense. (Circle one.) Why?

   _____

   _____

   _____

   _____

   _____

9. In the following words, indicate the vowel phoneme represented by each underlined letter or pair of letters.

d<u>a</u>nce	/____/	<u>aw</u>ful	/____/
d<u>ou</u>ble	/____/	<u>a</u>way	/____/
p<u>u</u>t	/____/	av<u>e</u>nge	/____/
d<u>i</u>sk	/____/	v<u>e</u>rse	/____/

10. In the following words, indicate the consonant phoneme represented by each underlined letter or pair of letters.

<u>g</u>in	/____/	<u>wh</u>ere	/____/
<u>g</u>oat	/____/	<u>ph</u>onics	/____/
<u>c</u>oat	/____/	lu<u>x</u>	/____/ / /____/
<u>w</u>ho	/____/	<u>c</u>ent	/____/

11. How many phonemes are represented in the following words? Write each word using its phoneme pronunciation symbols.

phone	____	_____
out	____	_____
knew	____	_____
about	____	_____

auto   _____   _____

could   _____   _____

toy   _____   _____

pearl   _____   _____

pudding   _____   _____

dare   _____   _____

12. Reading is a visual act that requires effective _____ vision.

13. _____ _____, the ability to hear sounds of varying pitch and loudness, is an important factor in beginning reading.

14. (True–False) Children who enter school with a knowledge of letter names are more likely to become better readers than children who lack this knowledge. Therefore, teaching children the letter names in kindergarten should eliminate many of our reading problems at the lower grade levels. Why?

_____

_____

_____

_____

_____

_____

15. Research indicates that practicing visual discrimination for reading is best accomplished through what kind of activities?

_____

_____

_____

POINTS TO PONDER: AN INVITATION TO DIALOGUE

16. With a partner, discuss the differences between the inductive and deductive approaches to teaching phonics.
17. How do the generalizations found in this chapter compare and contrast to the reading material used in your school? For preservice teachers, engage a teacher colleague regarding this question.
18. What teaching resources do you have that focus on the generalizations discussed in this chapter?
19. What does your state curriculum suggest is the appropriate grade level order of presentation of the phonics generalizations found in this chapter?
20. What should middle school and high school teachers know about these generalizations?

6 Teaching Consonants and Vowels

The most current basal reading series generally include a significant amount of phonics training at lower grade levels. An examination of the phonics content of current basal series leads to several observations:

1. The scope and sequence of phonics in basal series vary widely, and research has not identified the best sequence in which decoding skills should be taught. Consequently, decisions about the order of instruction are often related to the words used in the basal series' stories.

2. Formal instruction begins with an emphasis on initial consonant sounds. This practice appears logical because (a) consonant sounds are more consistent in their spelling than are vowel sounds and so are less confusing to children, (b) written English has a left-to-right orientation whereby the initial position of words assumes the most significant position in word recognition, and (c) most of the words that children are initially asked to learn begin with consonant sounds.

3. Although initial emphasis is placed on consonants, there is an early introduction (readiness, preprimer, and primer texts) of some vowels that allows children to decode meaningful words from the very early stages of reading instruction and provides them with skills that allow some degree of independence.

4. Practically all phonics content is taught by the end of second grade. With the advent of the No Child Left Behind Act and now Race to the Top, however, there has been a significant initiative to introduce phonics content knowledge traditionally taught in first grade into the kindergarten curriculum. This has resulted in earlier presentation of all phonics material at each successive grade level. The developmental appropriateness of this material for some children remains to be evaluated. Current research in language acquisition continues to support the notion that early language learning is more efficient when the elements of language children develop at home are reinforced in the elementary grades (Birdsong, 1999; Bongaerts, 2005; Brown, 2007; Gersten & Geva, 2003; Jedynak, 2009). The hypothesis that language acquisition ability diminishes dramatically during adolescence

and beyond seems to be tempered by another view of the process suggesting that the decay of language learning facility is a gradual but continuous process for most learners rather than a precipitous decline (Henning, McIntosh, Amott, & Dodd, 2010; Long, 2005). This would suggest that there is indeed a critical period for most first and second language learning that coincides with the traditional elementary grade levels (Nikolov, 2009; Singleton, 2005; Singleton & Lengyel, 1995; Singleton & Ryan, 2004). Policy makers and school districts seeking to have an impact on all language learners should consider assigning appropriate resources and personnel to the early elementary grades if the maximum impact on learning is to be realized (Arabski & Wojtaszek, Ashbrook, 2010; August & Shanahan, 2010; Song, 2006). In most basal series, only a few of the most difficult or infrequent letter–sound combinations are taught as late as third grade.

5. Most basal reading series include word patterns or *phonograms* at the start of their reading programs.

As shown by these observations, not all consonant sounds are taught before vowels are introduced. Remember that some consonants rarely occur in words and need not be addressed in beginning reading. In addition, every word has at least one vowel letter.

CONSONANTS

A review of the consonant phonemes is in order here. As discussed in Chapter 3, there are 25 consonant phonemes, 18 of which are composed of single letters and seven of which are composed of two-letter combinations. Fill in a key word that contains the sound of each two-letter phoneme.

/b/	bat	/ch/	_____
/d/	did	/hw/	_____
/f/	fat	/ng/	_____
/g/	go	/sh/	_____
/h/	he	/th/	_____
/j/	jam	/TH/	_____
/k/	kid	/zh/	_____
/l/	let		
/m/	me		
/n/	no		
/p/	pan		
/r/	run		

/s/	sat
/t/	ten
/v/	very
/w/	will
/y/	yes
/z/	zoo

Up to this point in the text, an instructional emphasis has been placed on learning phonemes. In teaching phonics, however, one begins with letters or graphemes and teaches children to recognize the sounds that correspond to them. The difficulty of this task is proportionately related to the level of consistency existing between letters and sounds. Because consonants are far more consistent in their spelling–sound relationships than are vowels, they are less confusing to children. Still, various problems arise when teaching consonants.

Single Consonants

Of the 21 consonant letters, 17 are basically phonemically consistent when they occur by themselves and not in combination (digraphs) with other letters. These include the following:

b   d   f   h   j   k   l   m   n   p   q   r   t   v   w   y   z

The four consonant letters that do not show a somewhat consistent one-to-one correspondence between letter and phoneme are *c, g, s,* and *x*. Each is discussed separately here.

The Letter *C*: *C* generally represents two phonemes, /k/ and /s/. (Remember, the letter *c* does not represent a phoneme identified by its own name.)

city	/s/	pact	/k/
coat	/k/	receive	/s/
rice	/s/	action	/k/

When the letter *c* represents /s/, it is commonly called the "soft c." When it represents /k/, it is commonly called the "hard c." Generally, the hard c is taught first because it occurs more frequently, especially as an initial letter in words.

The Letter *G*: *G* generally represents two phonemes, /g/ and /j/.

go	/g/	gull	/g/
gym	/j/	wage	/j/
agile	/j/	nag	/g/

When *g* represents /j/, it is commonly called the "soft g." When it represents /g/, it is commonly called the "hard g." Generally, the hard g is taught first for the same reasons that hard c is taught first: it occurs more frequently.

Double C and Double G

When consonants *c* and *g* are doubled within a word, frequently they record sounds that represent a combination of their hard and soft sound. In the word *suggest*, for example, the first g records its hard sound, while the second g records its soft sound. In *success*, the first c records its hard sound, and the second c records its soft sound.

The Letter *S:* *S* generally represents two phonemes, /s/ and /z/, with /s/ being taught first.

smile	/s/	his	/z/
season	/z/	tops	/s/
is	/z/	test	/s/

The Letter *X:* *X* generally represents three phonemes: /z/, /k/ /s/, and /g/ /z/. (Remember that *x* does not represent a phoneme that is identified by its own name.)

sox	/k/ /s/	expect	/k/ /s/
exit	/g/ /z/ or /k/ /s/	mix	/k/ /s/
anxiety	/g/ /z/	xerox	/z/

Although the most common single letter–sound relationships have been previously discussed and should be adequate for phonics instruction, there are many exceptions to consider. Fortunately, they occur infrequently. Here is a sampling of some of these exceptions:

of	/v/
individual	/j/
pleasure	/zh/
sure	/sh/
cello	/ch/
think	/ng/

Consonant Blends (Clusters)

Consonant blends are sounds in a syllable represented by two or more letters that are blended together *without* losing their own identity. Although blends are actually separate sounds, they are dealt with together because they occur frequently in syllables. It should be noted that 15 of the 21 initial consonant blend combinations contain either an *r* or an *l*. The letters *l* and *r* belong to the same sound family. Many languages do not differentiate between the sounds of *l* and *r*, and speakers of those languages cannot hear the difference when English speakers use them in the initial position of words. The /l/ sound is often inserted into words as beginning readers attempt to decode them aloud. The intrusive /l/ sound helps the beginning reader define the vowel sound articulated after it. The /r/ sound is also intrusive but less often. The tendency to insert /l/ and /r/ diminishes as the reader gains proficiency.

Initial consonant blends frequently taught in current basal series include the following:

br	fr	tr	fl	sc	sn	sw
cr	gr	bl	gl	sl	sp	spr
dr	pr	cl	pl	sm	st	str

Final consonant blends frequently taught in current basal series include the following:

-ld	(cold)	-lk (walk)	-nd (pond)	-nk (drink)	-nt (want)
-mp	(lamp)	-sk (ask)	-st (last)	-ft (lift)	-lt (colt)

Consonant Digraphs

To review, consonant digraphs consist of two letters that stand for a single phoneme. Several letter combinations are classified as consonant digraphs. In teaching phonics, however, a limited number of these digraphs must be taught. Children should learn either that some letter combinations represent a new sound that is different from the sound represented by each letter separately or that one of the two letters is silent. Although basals vary in the consonant digraphs they teach, the following occur most frequently:

Initial Consonant Digraphs

ch	(chubby)	ph	(phone)	wh	(why)
gn	(gnat)	sh	(she)	wr	(wrong)
kn	(known)	th	(the)		

Ending Consonant Digraphs

-ch	(lunch)	-gh	(tough)	-ng	(sing)
-ck	(luck)	-ll	(call)	-ss	(class)
-ff	(off)	-mb	(lamb)	-th	(teeth)

Of these consonant digraphs, *th* and *ch* create the most confusion because they are inconsistent and frequently represent more than one sound.

The Consonant Digraph *Th*: *Th* can represent one of two phonemes, /th/ or /TH/. One is called a voiceless sound (/th/) because, when spoken, air is expelled and little vibration is created by the voice box or tongue. Try the following voiceless /th/ sounds:

thing	thigh	thank	thumb
bath	ether	cloth	teeth

The other sound associated with the consonant digraph *th* is called a voiced sound (/TH/) because, when spoken, little air is expelled and a definite vibration is created in the voice box and by the tongue. Try the following voiced /TH/ sounds:

then	clothe	this	these
thy	their	bathe	either

When teaching the sounds associated with *th*, it is not necessary to burden children with the terms *voiceless* and *voiced*. Simply pointing out that *th* can represent one of two sounds as heard in designated key words will suffice.

The Consonant Digraph *Ch*: *Ch* usually represents the phoneme /ch/, as in *church*. Less frequently, *ch* represents the phoneme /k/, as in *chemical*, and the phoneme /sh/, as in *machine*.

VOWELS

Because of the inconsistent nature of the sounds that vowel letters represent, teaching vowel sounds is the most difficult task in phonics instruction. Because of this inconsistency, one must be careful to avoid any vowel instruction that will confuse rather than assist children in attacking unknown words. An examination of the phonics content of current basal series leads to several observations:

1. The scope and sequence of vowel instruction varies widely. Research has not identified the best sequence in which vowels should be taught.

2. Although formal instruction places initial emphasis on consonant sounds, vowels are introduced early. Vowel instruction is begun at either the readiness and preprimer text levels or the primer text level.

3. The greater part of vowel instruction up to first grade is devoted to short vowel sounds and long vowel sounds as represented by certain vowel digraphs (*ai, ay, ea, ee*) or words having the spelling pattern, vowel-consonant-*e* (i.e., *hope, take*).

4. Increased attention is being given to teaching vowel sounds within particular rimes as represented by phonograms. This approach takes advantage of the fact that vowel sounds are far more stable within particular rimes than they are in isolation.

5. The schwa sound is often introduced at approximately the second- or third-grade level. It is generally taught as the initial sound of a two-syllable word beginning with the letter *a*, such as *about*.

6. Instruction in some of the most difficult vowel digraphs and diphthongs is delayed until third grade.

A review of the 19 vowel phonemes follows:

/ā/	age	/ē/	ease	/ō/	ice	/ō/	old	/ū/	use
/ă/	an	/ĕ/	end	/ĭ/	in	/ŏ/	odd	/ŭ/	up
/oi/	oil (diphthong)	/ou/		out	(diphthong)				
/o͞o/	too	/o͝o/	good	/ə/	about				
/â/	dare	/û/	her	/ä/	father	/ô/	off		

As mentioned earlier in this chapter, when teaching phonics, one begins with letters or graphemes and teaches children to recognize the sounds that correspond to them. Because vowels are not consistent in their spellings, this becomes a formidable task.

Short–Long Vowel Sounds

Short vowel sounds are usually introduced in three-letter words with a spelling pattern of consonant-vowel-consonant (CVC). This is expanded to include words that follow the spelling patterns VC and CVCC. Several techniques can be used for formal instruction of short vowels. Two examples follow:

1. Using phonograms to build word families. For instance, using the phonogram *ig*, one could develop the following word family: big, dig, pig, fig, wig.

2. Changing the vowel sound in known words to make new words: big, bag; dig, dog; wig, wag.

In contrast to short vowels, long vowels are usually introduced in words with a spelling pattern of VCe, as in *whale*. This is expanded to include certain vowel digraphs (*oa* in *boat*) and single-syllable words ending in a vowel (*o* in *go*).

Children are often taught or led to discover generalizations that will assist them in identifying short and long vowel sounds. The following examples are from basal series and illustrate varied approaches.

Silver Burdett Ginn (1993): "Say these words, elongating the vowel sound as you say each one: *man, pet, pin, nod, tub*. Point out that these words all have short vowel sounds. Say these words: *mane, Pete, pine, rode, tube*. Explain that these words all have long vowel sounds. Write each set of words on the chalkboard and have children compare both sets. Lead them to see that short vowel words have a consonant-vowel-consonant pattern and long vowel words have a consonant-vowel-consonant-*e* pattern" (p. T71).

Houghton Mifflin (1997c): "Have children read the first two sentences on page 10 with you. Ask them to listen for the vowel sounds in *no* and *mop*. Write the words on the chalkboard. Ask these questions:

What vowel sound do you hear in *mop*? (short *o*)

Do you hear the same vowel sound in *no*? (*no*)

Remind children that the vowel sound in *no* is the long *o* sound. Label the CV pattern in *no*. You may also want to have children contrast these words: not-no; got-go" (p. T69).

Vowel Digraphs

Vowel digraphs are two-vowel letters that stand for a single sound or phoneme. Several letter combinations are classified as vowel digraphs. In teaching phonics, however, only a limited number of these digraphs must be taught because many vowel digraphs are not consistent enough in their spelling–sound relationships to justify teaching them.

An analysis of current basal series reveals that most include instruction for the following vowel digraphs:

Vowel Digraphs	Phonemes
ee, ea	/ē/
ai, ay	/ā/
oa, ow	/ō/
Oo	/ōo/
Oo	/ŏo/
ou, ow	/ou/ (diphthong)
oi, oy	/oi/ (diphthong)
au, aw	/ô/

In teaching vowel digraphs, basals tend to emphasize the most common sound represented by specific digraph combinations. These basals also point out that some vowel digraphs (*oi, oy, ou, ow, oo*) are special cases and represent sounds that are neither long nor short.

R-Controlled Vowels

Children are taught that when a vowel is followed by the consonant letter *r*, the vowel sound is neither short nor long:

Read aloud the sentence on page 18 and point out the word *shark*. Explain that when a vowel is followed by an *r*, the vowel sound is neither long nor short, and that the letters *ar* often stand for the vowel sound heard in *shark*.

Ask children to look on page 19 and find three other words in which *ar* stands for the sound heard in *shark* (*are, far, apart*).

Next, explain that the sound for *o* followed by *r* is neither long nor short. Ask a volunteer to read page 20. Point to *for* and explain that the letters *or* often stand for the vowel sound in *for* (Houghton Mifflin, 1997a, p. T257).

Intrusive L and R Sounds

Teachers often notice that the beginning readers in their classrooms insert the sound /l/ or the sound /r/ where they do not belong in a word. The word *gill* becomes *grill*, for example. Or the word *sing* becomes *sling*. These "added sounds" are interesting to observe and think about because they represent a phenomenon related to the class of sounds to which the letters *l* and *r* belong, called *approximates.* In many languages, especially tonal languages such as Chinese and syllabic languages such as Japanese, the sounds of /l/ and /r/ are allophones. An allophone is a phonetic variant of a phoneme, and it can manifest itself with varying sounds. As strange as it might seem to speakers of English, many speakers of other languages do not hear or make distinctions between the /l/ sound and the /r/ sound, making the process of producing these English phonemes difficult for some L2 learners. The transition to writing and learning to spell can also be difficult; sequentially misplacing the letters *l* or *r* within a word for beginning spellers is also common, as in "The gril was walking down the street" rather than "The girl was walking down the street." Other languages such as Spanish, for example, have additional variants for the sounds /l/ and /r/ that also vary from English pronunciation norms. It is important for teachers to be aware of the articulation differences inherent in the production of the /l/ and /r/ sounds for both L1 and L2 learners. The sounds of /l/ and /r/ are generally problematic within a wide range of languages, not just English (Jumulowicz, 2009; Lems & Soro, 2010; Manchon, 2009).

The Schwa Sound

The schwa sound is introduced at approximately the second- or third-grade level and is often taught in conjunction with syllabication and/or dictionary use. Although the schwa sound may be represented by any of the vowel letters, little attention is given to the teaching of the schwa sound despite the fact that it is the most common vowel sound in English.

A schwa is a short, unstressed vowel that often occurs in unaccented syllables. Therefore, children would have to divide words into proper syllables, identify which syllables are unaccented, and finally determine which vowels are schwas. Obviously, this systematic approach is beyond the capabilities of young children. Little instructional attention, therefore, is given to teaching children how to decode the schwa sound in a technical, systematic manner. Fortunately, since the schwa sound is a soft vowel sound that is similar to the short *u* sound, children often come close enough to the sound to render a correct pronunciation in their decoding attempts.

Teaching Vowels Through Phonograms

Wylie and Durrell (1970) conducted a study showing that the following 37 phonograms can be combined with various consonant letters to generate approximately 500 primary words:

-ack	-ail	-ain	-ake	-ale	-ame	-an
-ank	-ap	-ash	-at	-ate	-aw	-ay
-eat	-ell	-est	-ice	-ick	-ide	-ight
-ill	-in	-ine	-ing	-ink	-ip	-it
-ock	-oke	-op	-ore	-ot	-uck	-ug
-ump	-unk					

Wylie and Durrell (1970) found that children learned the vowel sounds contained in phonograms more easily compared to learning these sounds through individual letter–sound correspondences or phonic generalizations.

CHAPTER 6: PRACTICE

1. The inconsistent spelling of (consonant sounds, vowel sounds) is a basic problem of phonics. (Circle one.)

2. There are _____ vowel phonemes in the English language.

3. The _____ sound is a short, unstressed vowel that often occurs in unaccented syllables.

4. There (is, is not) a best sequence in which vowels should be taught. (Circle one.)

5. Of the 21 single consonant letters, four are phonemically inconsistent and represent more than one sound. Alphabetically list these four consonant letters, indicate the phonemes they can represent, and write out a key word for each.

Letter	Phonemes	Words	
_____	/__/, /__/	_____ ,	_____
_____	/__/, /__/	_____ ,	_____
_____	/__/, /__/	_____ ,	_____
_____	/__/	_____	
	/__/ /__/	_____	
	/__/ /__/	_____	

6. The "soft c" is represented by the phoneme /__/.

   The "hard c" is represented by the phoneme /__/.

   The "soft g" is represented by the phoneme /__/.

   The "hard g" is represented by the phoneme /__/.

7. (Consonant digraphs, Consonant blends) are sounds in a syllable represented by two or more letters that are combined without losing their individual identity. (Circle one.)

8. Can you discriminate between consonant digraphs and consonant blends? Write D after letter combinations that represent digraphs and B after letter combinations that represent blends.

br _____   pl _____   -ck _____   -sk _____

ch _____   sh _____   -nk _____   -ld _____

cl _____   wh _____   -mp _____   -ng _____

kn _____   pr _____   -mb _____   -st _____

th _____   gr _____   -nt _____   -nd _____

9. Short and long vowels are often introduced in words with certain spelling patterns. Are the following patterns short or long?

CVC   _____

CV   _____

VCe   _____

VC   _____

10. What is the advantage of teaching vowel sounds within phonograms as compared to teaching them in isolation?

_____

_____

_____

_____

11. Why should teacher and material resources be allocated to the development of first and second language programs within the elementary school grades?

_____

_____

_____

_____

12. What are some of the implications of delaying the onset of second language instruction for L2 children?

_____

_____

_____

_____

13. Phonics instruction usually begins with (consonant sounds, vowel sounds). (Circle one.)

14. The _____ sound is the most common vowel sound in English.

15. An allophone is (a sound belonging to the same phoneme, a rhyming phoneme).
    (Circle one.)

16. The consonant letter _____ and the consonant letter _____ and their respective associated sounds tend to be inserted into words where they do not belong.

17. The decline of language acquisition skills occurs (gradually, precipitously) during the developmental period.
    (Circle one.)

CUMULATIVE REVIEW: CHAPTERS 1 TO 6

1. Phonics (appears, does not appear) to be the panacea for most reading ills.
   (Circle one.)

2. Phonics instruction should be completed by the end of _____ grade for most children.

3. Define the following terms:

   Phonics:

   _____

   _____

   _____

   Phoneme:

   _____

   _____

   _____

   Open syllable:

   _____

   _____

   _____

   Macron:

   _____

   _____

   _____

Consonant:

_____

_____

_____

Digraph:

_____

_____

_____

Syllable:

_____

_____

_____

4. Underline any consonant or vowel digraph contained in the following words:

out   book   blunt   stun   that

dare   song   chat   knob   clip

5. A _____ of two letters is called a digraph.

6. Fill in the proper consonant phoneme for each of the following underlined letter(s):

c̲age	/__/	q̲ueen	/__/ /__/
w̲ho	/__/	sox̲	/__/ /__/
k̲new	/__/	c̲ell	/__/
measu̲re	/__/	cri̲tique	/__/

7. Fill in the proper vowel phoneme for each of the underlined letter(s):

a̲ir	/__/	to̲e	/__/
sena̲tor	/__/	ca̲ll	/__/
o̲tter	/__/	hou̲se	/__/
tu̲rn	/__/	goo̲d	/__/

8. How many phonemes are represented in the following words? Write each word using its phoneme pronunciation symbols.

red   _____   _____

coat   _____   _____

wheel   _____   _____

quit _____ _____

who _____ _____

when _____ _____

fly _____ _____

curse _____ _____

dialect _____ _____

9. What is emergent literacy, and how does it affect learning to read once children enter school?

_____

_____

_____

_____

_____

_____

10. Studies have shown that children who begin their schooling knowing the ABCs are more likely to become better readers than children who lack this knowledge. Of what importance is this fact for teachers of beginning reading?

_____

_____

_____

_____

_____

11. Write out the vowel generalization that the words below follow:
coat:

_____

_____

_____

hope:

_____

_____

_____

she:

_____

_____

_____

but:

_____

_____

_____

12. Why is it more effective to teach vowel *generalizations* than vowel *rules*?

_____

_____

_____

_____

_____

POINTS TO PONDER: AN INVITATION TO DIALOGUE

13. With another educator, discuss the ramifications of your school's policies on first and second language learning. How do these policies affect the way children learn in your classroom?

14. Who is responsible in your school district for disseminating information about bilingual education? What types of support do they offer classroom teachers with bilingual children in their classroom?

15. How much training have you had to work with bilingual children in your classroom during your undergraduate preservice training or within your school district?

16. If you teach in a bilingual classroom, what are some of your experiences with working with multilingual children?

7 Syllabication and Accenting

At first glance, especially for those who are competent readers, the process of syllabication appears to be a somewhat simple task. On closer examination, however, it reveals itself to be a rather complex process that many children find quite difficult. Why, then, should the process be taught to children? The answer lies in the fact that unless some systematic procedure is used when attempting to decode multisyllabic words, the process essentially becomes one of trial and error. Providing children with strategies for syllabication facilitates a more systematic approach to decoding unknown words; even though a certain amount of trial and error will remain, it becomes less random and more directed (Baron, 1999; Dilberto, Beattie, Flowers, & Algozzine, 2008; Marchand, Adset, & Damper, 2009; Rogers, DeMasi, & Krause, 2010).

A *syllable* is a basic unit of pronunciation consisting of a vowel alone or a vowel with one or more consonants. There is one—and only one—sounded vowel (phoneme) in each syllable. Phonic generalizations pertain to syllables, not to words, which means that syllables, not words, are initially decoded. For this reason, the vowel generalizations presented in Chapter 5 were stated in terms of syllables (Mattys & Melhorn, 2005; Rogers & Lopez, 2008; Smith, 2000).

As children begin to work with an increasing number of unknown polysyllabic words, they first must be able to syllabicate them correctly before applying vowel generalizations. Since they cannot divide unknown words by sound, they must rely on certain spelling patterns and/or generalizations to assist them in this task.

Before children are taught syllabication strategies or generalizations, they must learn the prerequisite skills of hearing and recognizing syllables in words, understanding letter–sound relationships, and knowing the useful phonic generalizations. It is not unusual, then, for the topic of syllabication to be introduced as late as the second or third grade.

Children are commonly introduced to syllabication by getting them to hear syllables in words they already know. The activity of clapping each syllable as they say words is often used at this introductory stage of instruction. Although it is appropriate to have children practice syllabication with known words at the onset of instruction when the concept is introduced, it is inappropriate to have children continue to practice their syllabication skills only on known words. To be effective, reinforcement and practice must be done using unknown words. Therefore, the practice items offered in this chapter consist mostly of nonsense words. These will encourage the mature readers of this text to experience and use the strategies and generalizations that their students will need to use when they attempt to decode unknown multisyllabic words. Syllabication generalizations that should assist children in their attempts to decode multisyllabic words include the following.

1. Every syllable contains one—and only one—vowel sound, but this vowel sound may be graphically represented by more than one vowel grapheme. This concept is best developed by helping children recognize syllables in words they already know. This task is accomplished through providing children with varied opportunities to hear and recognize syllables in spoken words. Eventually, children should be able to pronounce familiar words in syllabic form. Once children understand the concept of syllabication and know letter–sound relationships and appropriate phonic generalizations, attention turns to an analysis of word structure and the spelling patterns of words.

2. Most affixes (prefixes and suffixes) are syllables. Children are taught to look first for common word parts (prefixes and suffixes) that they have learned previously. Some of the most common prefixes and suffixes follow:

Prefix

dis-	in-	non-	sub-
em-	inter-	over-	un-
en-	ir-	pre-	
im-	mis-	re-	

Suffix

-able	-est	-ly	-y
-al	-ful	-ment	
-en	-ing	-ness	
-er	-less	-ion (-tion)	

Often, more specific generalizations related to affixes are taught as follows:

a. *-ture* and *-tion* are syllables (e.g., pic-ture, ma-ture, cap-tion, lo-tion).

b. The inflected *-ed* adds a syllable when affixed to a verb ending in *-d* or *-t*. Otherwise, it does not add a syllable (e.g., need-ed, root-ed, stayed, asked).

3. In a compound word, the syllabic division usually comes between the words of which it is composed. Divided compound words can be syllabicated according to other generalizations.

4. When a word ends in *-le* preceded by a consonant, the consonant plus *-le* make up a syllable (e.g., mid-dle, ar-ti-cle). It also usually contains a schwa sound.

5. When two vowel letters appear together, they usually represent one sound and should be viewed as a single grapheme when syllabicating. Burmeister (1966) examined the validity of this generalization using randomly selected words from the *Teacher's Word Book of 30,000 Words* (Thorndike & Lorge, 1944) and found that 84.5% of the time it proved true. In addition, one-third

of the exceptions occurred when the vowel pair *ia* appeared in words such as *giant*.

6. Letters representing consonant digraphs, especially *th, ch,* and *sh,* and consonant blends are treated as single consonants and are not separated when words are broken into syllables.

7. Although double consonant letters are generally separated when words are broken into syllables via writing, the sound will be represented in only one syllable as follows:

common	com-mon	kŏm-n
latter	lat-ter	lăt-ər
connote	con-note	kə-nōt

Once the specific generalizations previously described are addressed, the following generalizations are applied:

8. When two consonant letters are between two vowel letters, a syllabic division often occurs between the consonants. A current basal series expresses this generalization as follows: "Most VCCV words are divided into syllables between the consonants" (Houghton Mifflin, 1997b, p. 323E).

9. When there is one consonant letter between two vowel letters, the consonant often goes with the next syllable. This generalization has less consistency than does the previous statement regarding two consonants between two vowels (see Table 5.1, numbers 38 and 39). For this reason, basals usually present options as follows: "Most VCV words with the short-vowel pattern in the first syllable are divided after the consonant because the consonant is part of the short-vowel pattern. Most VCV words with a long-vowel sound or a *schwa* sound in the first syllable are divided before the consonant" (Houghton Mifflin, 1997b, p. 323E). Thus, students are told when they attempt to figure out an unfamiliar word syllable by syllable that they "might have to make several attempts, trying different pronunciations and stressing different syllables, before coming up with a word that sounds familiar" (Houghton Mifflin, 1997b, p. 323E).

In terms of accenting, two generalizations should suffice:

1. In two-syllable words, the accent is usually on the first syllable.

2. Prefixes and suffixes are generally not accented.

As you teach children generalizations that apply to syllabication and accenting, it is important to teach the concept that these provide a starting point in their attempts to decode words. If students' efforts yield words that do not make sense or are unknown, alternative efforts should be attempted. Teachers should no longer attempt to teach these generalizations as though they were *rules* that produce results without failure.

CHAPTER 7: PRACTICE

1. In a two-syllable word, the accent is usually on the _____ syllable.

2. Every syllable contains one—and only one— _____ sound.

3. Most affixes (are, are not) syllables. (Circle one.)

4. The inflected -ed adds a syllable when affixed to a verb that ends with either the letter _____ or _____.

5. When a word ends in -le preceded by a consonant, the consonant plus -le make up a syllable. When -le is preceded by a vowel, the e is usually

   _____.

6. Letters representing consonant digraphs, especially th, ch, and sh, and consonant blends are treated as single consonants and (are, are not) separated when words are broken into syllables. (Circle one.)

7. When two vowel letters appear together, they usually represent _____ sound.

8. When two consonant letters are between two vowel letters, a syllabic division often occurs _____ _____ _____.

9. In writing, double consonant letters are usually broken up into separate syllables. In speech, how is the pronunciation of double consonants handled?

   _____

   _____

   _____

   _____

   _____

   _____

   _____

10. Identify the syllabic divisions (as occurs in writing) in the following vowel–consonant letter patterns, nonsense words, or words. There are no consonant digraphs in the first seven letter patterns. In the space provided, indicate which generalization(s) you used to accomplish this task.

    ### Vowel-Consonant Letter Patterns

VCV	_____
VCCV	_____
VCVC	_____
CVCCV	_____
CCVCCVC	_____

CCVCVC _____

VCe _____   (Special VCV when final letter is *e*)

Real Words

amass _____   _____

aphis _____   _____

beldam _____   _____

retable _____   _____

bolide _____   _____

cupule _____   _____

foxed _____   _____

furbelow _____   _____

judicature _____   _____

Nonsense Words

preanthema _____   _____

unboted _____   _____

emakle _____   _____

epeture _____   _____

grapeet _____   _____

resired _____   _____

ecad _____   _____

antole _____   _____

scrnt _____   _____

mashot _____   _____

haulm _____   _____

subtonen _____   _____

CUMULATIVE REVIEW: CHAPTERS 1 TO 7

1. There (are, are not) significant research data that show the importance of phonics in beginning reading instruction. (Circle one.)

2. The latest research suggests the advantages of systematic synthetic phonics instruction (outweigh, do not outweigh) the disadvantages. (Circle one.)

3. Circle each of the following terms that refers to a letter or letters:

   phoneme vowel grapheme rime diphthong digraph consonant onset phonogram

4. Besides *a, e, i, o,* and *u,* what other two letters sometimes represent vowels? _____ and _____.

5. Circle each of the following words that contains a closed syllable:

   gone   so   sew   dove   tire   dough

6. Underline any consonant digraph contained in the following words:

   blade   ring   that   steel   shucks   chain   tree

7. Underline any vowel digraphs contained in the following words:

   few   good   feet   dove   oil   soup   letter

8. Phoneme _____ is the ability to isolate all sounds of a word.

9. The phonogram is the graphic representation of a _____.

10. The phonemes /oi/ and /ou/ are examples of a _____.

11. There are _____ phonemes in the English language, _____ consonant sounds, and _____ vowel sounds.

12. Circle the words that contain the /$\overline{oo}$/ sound:

    too   good   room   shoes   stood   look

13. The letters ___ , ___ , and ___ do not represent phonemes that are identified by their own names.

14. A single vowel letter in a syllable usually represents the short sound if

    _____

    _____

15. When two successive vowel letters occur in a syllable and they are not any of the special digraphs, the first usually records its _____ sound and the second is _____.

16. Fill in the proper vowel or consonant phoneme for each underlined letter(s).

    plaid   /____/   pleasure   /____/
    mare   /____/   long   /____/
    sky   /____/   basic   /____/
    toy   /____/   ghost   /____/

17. When a cumulative file contains information indicating a child has successfully passed a vision test, why might this information be misleading?

    _____

    _____

    _____

    _____

    _____

18. What relationship appears to exist between oral language and reading achievement?

_____

_____

_____

_____

_____

19. What is the difference between phoneme segmentation and phoneme blending? Provide an example of each approach.

_____

_____

_____

_____

_____

_____

20. Workbooks and other paper-and-pencil activities require students to learn or practice phonics silently. Is this an effective approach? Why?

_____

_____

_____

_____

_____

21. What is the difference between a synthetic (explicit) approach to teaching phonics and an analytical (implicit) approach?

_____

_____

_____

_____

_____

_____

22. Formal instruction in phonics usually begins with an emphasis on initial _____ sounds. Why?

_____

_____

_____

_____

_____

_____

_____

23. Identify a phonogram and indicate how to instructionally develop a word family.

_____

_____

_____

_____

_____

_____

24. How does the ability to syllabicate words assist children in their attempts to pronounce unknown words?

_____

_____

_____

_____

_____

_____

25. Define the following terms.

Phonetics:

_____

_____

_____

_____

_____

Grapheme:

_____

_____

_____

Vowels:

_____

_____

_____

Diphthong:

_____

_____

_____

Consonant blend:

_____

_____

_____

Rime:

_____

_____

_____

Schwa:

_____

_____

_____

POINTS TO PONDER: AN INVITATION TO DIALOGUE

26. With another educator, discuss syllable activities used in your classrooms. Which of the activities by grade level seem to make the most sense to your learners?

27. In teaching syllabication, what are some of the nonverbal ways—clapping syllables, for example—that you have used in your classroom?

28. Supersegmentals are aspects of language such as stress, pitch, and intonation. How might you use these three language components to better teach syllable division?

8 Diagnostic Teaching

The goal of every teacher should be to provide an environment in which children are allowed the opportunity to grow toward their full potential. This learning environment can be accomplished only if teachers are able to identify the individual strengths and weaknesses of students and can develop instructional strategies that take advantage of this knowledge. In essence, it requires every classroom teacher to participate in diagnostic teaching.

To assume this diagnostic role effectively, teachers need to become aware of the general principles of diagnosis as well as the elements of diagnosis related to specific content areas. Discussion of both the general principles of diagnosis and the specific procedures for diagnosing phonics follow.

GENERAL PRINCIPLES OF DIAGNOSIS

General diagnostic principles include the following:

1. Diagnosis should be viewed as a daily occurrence. In fact, since the advent of the No Child Left Behind Act and the Race to the Top initiative, frequently teachers are required to gather explicit data on the five elements of reading set out in the National Reading Panel's report. In the case of letter knowledge and phonemic awareness, specific classroom assessments such as DIBELS and assessments found within the basal reading series used in the classroom are now mandated by districts and state boards of education (Dessoff, 2007; Goffreda & DiPerna, 2010; Nelson, 2008; Riedel & Samuels, 2007). Lesson scripting, teaching with fidelity, benchmarks, and mandatory state curricula have necessitated that the classroom teacher keep accurate, continuous diagnostic records for each student. Accountability measures for improvement in Annual Yearly Progress Reports issued by districts and state boards of education have led to the firing of teachers, reconstitution of schools that do not meet Annual Yearly Progress benchmarks, and the involuntary reassignment of teachers to other schools. It is for this reason and many others that teachers take the business of reading diagnosis seriously, especially in the early elementary classrooms where reading curriculum once reserved for first grade is now being taught in preschool and kindergarten. Reading diagnosis is no longer treated as a special event that takes place only once or twice a year.

In reality, teachers now observe and evaluate children on a continuing basis because children's needs and/or skills can change drastically over a short period of time (Ross, 2004; Scott & Christ, 2009; Smith et al., 2008).

2. Decisions about children should be based on diagnostic information collected from various sources. Instructional decisions about children should never be made on the basis of a single test or observation, and these decisions must be based on facts, not opinions. Generally speaking, the more diverse the data that the teacher collect is, the more useful the information becomes when targeting instruction for a specific need of the learner.

3. The identification of patterns of errors should be emphasized when analyzing diagnostic information. If a type of error occurs in a pattern, greater confidence can be placed on the interpretation that the error is truly a problem for the child. When decisions are based on isolated errors, unneeded instruction and practice often follow. Horizontal assessments, or assessments conducted over multiple learning events, provide the teacher with a clearer picture of the contexts of the reading errors and help the teacher to sharpen responses to them.

4. Instruction should focus on only one or two reading weaknesses at a time. In the process of reading diagnosis, a teacher frequently finds that the child exhibits several significant reading weaknesses. If attempts are made to remediate all these weaknesses at once, it generally overwhelms the child and further frustrates his or her efforts to improve. Narrow the skills to be taught to the one or two that appear to create the most difficulty and remediate these before continuing with others that are less debilitating. Beginning teachers and clinicians frequently express concern about knowing where to begin the process of diagnosis and remediation. Usually this is because of lack of experience within the diagnostic and remedial process. It is important to point out that often children and adults who are learning to read have a great deal of insight into their own reading difficulties and are quite willing to share their perceptions if we are careful to listen. Encouraging dialog with and careful observation of the reader in the process of working with meaningful reading material is good diagnostic practice.

5. Diagnosis for its own sake is not acceptable; it must lead to specific instructional action. Teachers must avoid becoming so enamored of the diagnostic process that they lose sight of the ultimate objective of diagnosis—the identification and remediation of weaknesses or disabilities. An exception to this principle occurs when preservice teachers or clinical practicum students are learning to administer informal reading inventories or other diagnostic measures. In this case, some amount of practice and expertise using the instrument is required, but as stated earlier, it is extremely important that the material is meaning-centered.

The procedures for evaluating phonic skills are varied and include both informal and formal diagnosis. The following is a sample of procedures teachers can use and items they can construct to assist them in diagnosing students' phonic skills.

PROCEDURES FOR DIAGNOSING PHONIC SKILLS

Observation

During a typical school day, teachers have many opportunities to observe and collect pertinent information about the reading proficiencies of students. To take advantage of these opportunities, teachers need to devise written systems that allow them to record their observations over time. In fact, most school districts now require teachers to conduct some form of running records with all children in their classrooms. While the frequency and number of required records per child varies, they have become a fact of life for most teachers. These records, in turn, can be analyzed later to identify weaknesses or patterns of error. In some cases the results of the running records are reported to the administration in the teacher's school or to the school improvement team or its counterpart. Running records are usually teacher-produced reading samples that are coded while an individual reader reads aloud, but school districts are moving toward commercially based running records that are closely tied to the basal reading series used within the classroom and school (Ross, 2004). Because running records are designed for efficient classroom application and generally take less time than traditional reading inventories, it is typical for teachers to conduct multiple running records for each child in their classes during the school year. These observations can also be used to verify or question results gathered through more formalized data collections (Deeney, 2010; Fawson, Ludlow, Reutzel, Dweeks, & Smith, 2006; Johnson, Jenkins, Yaacov, & Catts, 2009; Mather, Sammons, & Schwartz, 2006; Moore & Seeger, 2010; Wurr, Theurer, & Kim, 2008).

There is no best way to collect and categorize observational data. This process can be as simple as developing a file for each child and recording observations by date as they occur, similar to the system used by medical doctors. Or teachers may construct more specific observational documents to identify the exact phonic skills to be observed. For example, if one of the skills a teacher decides to analyze is the ability to pronounce initial consonants correctly in single-syllable words, the teacher can simply construct a sheet with the consonant letters listed on it and mark them off as children pronounce each consonant. Teachers can observe and/or develop recording sheets related to phonic elements such as single-letter consonant sounds, double-letter consonant sounds, consonant blends, long vowels, short vowels, r-controlled vowels, diphthongs, vowel combinations (especially *ee, ea, ai, ay, oa*), double *o*, knowledge of vowel and consonant generalizations, phoneme segmentation, and phoneme blending.

Informal Reading Inventory

The informal reading inventory (IRI) is a more formal procedure for observing, recording, and analyzing children's reading proficiencies. Generally, these inventories attempt to measure, through the oral reading of a set of graded word lists and paragraphs, both word recognition and comprehension skills of those taking the test. As the examinee reads the word lists and paragraphs for the word recognition part of the inventory, all errors or reading miscues are recorded on a sheet that is later used to analyze and categorize the types of errors or miscues the examinee made (similar to the teacher's written comments mentioned in the previous section on observation). An important distinction needs to be drawn between the terms *error* and *miscue*. Psycholinguists, those who study and apply the relationship between the psychological processing aspects of reading and the linguistic components that support them, refer to a set of cueing systems employed by readers as they read. In their perspective, an "error" while reading actually reflects a misapplication of one of the cueing systems. The significance of this difference is important because psycholinguists understand that miscues help teachers to get glimpses into the thought processes of the reader (Farrington, 2007; Garcia, 2007; McKenna, 2006). In the view of psycholinguists, miscues are neither random nor meaningless. Analysis of miscues, they believe, helps teachers to understand deep connections between readers and the texts they are reading (Goodman, 1969). For example, the grapho-phonemic cueing system, which is a substantive component of what you have been learning in this book, addresses the relationship between graphemes and the sounds they represent in English. Since miscue analysis is frequently a component of the process of developing and applying running records in the classroom, it is important to recognize the contributions that psycholinguistics has made to this analytic process. However, the chief focus of earlier systems of miscue analysis was largely upon the syntactic and semantic cueing systems as opposed to the grapho-phonemic cueing system. The emphasis was less on phonemic awareness and more on whole language learning and its concomitant reliance on syntax and meaning to guide the reader (Spear-Swerling, 2007; Vanderwood, Linklater, & Healy, 2008).

Running records and other forms of informal reading inventories have certain limitations that teachers should recognize. They can be administered to only one person at a time and require a significant amount of time to administer and analyze. For these reasons, many reading authorities feel it is impractical to recommend that the IRI be administered to every child in a class despite the fact that teachers are frequently required to do so. Rather, it might best be administered to those who are having significant problems in reading and about whom teachers feel they need more information. Another limitation that must be recognized is the fact that data from an IRI are but one sample of behavior that has been gathered at a specific point in time. The data may or may not be representative of the child's real skills. Therefore, even if an IRI is given, the data should be tested by comparing the results to data gathered through teacher observations and other evaluative procedures (Coulter, 2009).

Several standardized tests fall under the category of informal reading inventories. Some that are common in the field include the following:

Analytical Reading Inventory, Sixth Edition, by Mary Lynn Woods and Alden J. Moe. (1999). Upper Saddle River, NJ: Prentice Hall.

Basic Reading Inventory, 10th Edition, by Jerry L. Johns. (2009). Dubuque, IA: Kendall/Hunt.

Classroom Reading Inventory, Seventh Edition, by Nicholas J. Silvaroli. (1994). Dubuque, IA: Brown & Benchmark.

Diagnosis and Remediation in the Multilingual Classroom

One of the significant changes occurring in the classroom today is the arrival of students whose first language is not English (Bhatia & Ritchie, 2006). This trend presents challenges and opportunities to teachers for reading and language instruction. Even a cursory examination of the field of bilingual education and the research that supports it demonstrates that new sets of concerns arise related to how best to teach these learners. Earlier in this text it was suggested that teachers adopt and model three specific teaching characteristics, mentoring, translating, and guiding. Nowhere is the importance of these roles seen more clearly than in the multilingual classroom. Being a "translator" might literally mean that the teacher employs teaching strategies based on the reader's native language. In large urban school districts it is not unusual for dozens of different languages to be spoken in the schools. When these languages are based on alphabetic systems—Spanish, for example—the transition to English phoneme and grapheme relationships may be assisted by prior knowledge of the first (L1) or native language as it applies to the acquisition of the L2 language, which in this case is English. This assumes, however, that beginning readers know from the start the phoneme-grapheme relationship of their native languages. It is entirely possible that beginning readers entering today's classrooms do not know the relationship between phonemes and graphemes in their native languages, regardless of whether or not they are based on an alphabetic system. If English is not spoken at home, beginning readers receive no reinforcement for what is being taught in school (Duursma et al., 2007; Ferris, 2006). If their native language is not spoken in school, they receive no reinforcement for all the rich aspects represented by that language. This is one reason why school children become illiterate in two languages (DeCapua, Smathers, & Tang, 2007; Echevarria & Graves, 2007; Gallo, Garcia, Pinuelas, & Youngs, 2008; Graves, Plasencia-Peinado, Deno, & Johnson, 2005; Menken & Kleyn, 2010).

Language and identity are closely related (Huhtala & Lehti-Eklund, 2010). If language learning was simply a matter of learning the sounds and the graphemes that represent them, our task would be relatively simple. But language learning is not that simple. Language represents culture in all its myriad aspects and diversity. To strip learners of these connections is to impoverish them in some deeply important ways. Acquiring a second language is to become aware of a whole set of additional cultural perspectives, some of which may conflict with the values and mores of learners' native cultures (Santamaria, 2009; Thu, 2010; Tokuhama-Espinosa, 2001). While the chief focus of this text is phonics, it is important to understand that phonics is not taught in a cultural vacuum. How we teach phonics can be as important as what we teach and when we teach it (Calhoon, Otaiba, Cihak, King, & Avalos, 2007; DelliCarpini, 2010). There are many intriguing cultural differences that bear on successful teaching in the multilingual classroom. Some cultures encourage and prize direct eye contact between speakers and listeners; others do not (Navarra & Soto-Faraco, 2007).

As a mode of learning, some cultures place high emphasis on being able to see the lips of the speaker when learning to read; others do not (Grinstead, 2009; Gyovai, Cartledge, Kourea, Yurick, & Gibson, 2009; Jeynes, 2008). The following recommendations and the resources associated with them are intended to provide a beginning point for the application of reading diagnosis as it applies to phonics instruction within the multilingual classroom.

1. *Teach phonics explicitly.* All learners, regardless of their first language, need specific, targeted information about the sound–symbol relationships of English to succeed in reading (Byrd, 2008; Linan-Thompson, Vaughn, Prater, & Cirino, 2006; Macaro, 2006; Manyak, 2008; Rycik, 2007; Wernham, 2005).

2. *Know the cultures of the children in your classroom.* If you are to provide a bridge between the native languages of the children in your multilingual classroom and the world of words and meanings in English, it is imperative that you understand and respect the cultures of the children you are teaching (Leaux, 2010; Lesauk, Kieffer, Faller, & Kelly, 2010; Manyak, 2007).

3. *Use a wide range of teaching approaches and strategies.* Children learn in different ways; a one-size-fits-all model will not work for all children in your classroom (Chappell, 2008; Gerber et al., 2004; Malloy, Gilbertson, & Maxfield, 2007; Mayer & Leigh, 2010; McIntosh, Graves, & Gersten, 2007; McMaster, Kung, Han, & Cao, 2008; Schmitt, 2001).

4. *Think aloud.* Modeling thinking and problem solving aloud while teaching phonics, or any other subject for that matter, is extremely useful (Beverly, Giles, & Buck, 2009; Miller et al., 2006; Millett, Atwill, Blanchard, & Gorin, 2008; Strid & Booth, 2007).

5. *Actively use language in your classroom.* Research demonstrates that L2 children benefit when teachers actively use language with them that is meaningful and highly related to the processes required for successful membership in the classroom setting (Brown, 2009; Cox & Hopkins, 2006; Duffy, 2003).

6. *Use meaningful reading material.* Understanding what we read motivates further reading (Eslami-Rasekh, 2005; Goh, 2008; Walqui & Van Lier, 2010).

7. *Model and teach tolerance.* As discussed earlier, language is intimately related to the identity of the speakers who use it. The inherent message in teaching L2s English can become a political event where the primary or native language is demeaned or unnecessarily subordinated to the teaching of English phonics. Look for linguistic bridges of similarities and differences that provide opportunities for the development of linguistic competence without prejudice (Ferris, 2006; Hones, Aquilar, & Thao, 2009; Kamps et al., 2007; Kroll & De Groot, 2005; Vaughn et al., 2006).

8. *Adopt and value dialogue as a teaching style.* Monologues, or one-sided conversations, do not invite participation and ownership of the ideas being presented. The use of a monologue style of teaching in the classroom may be experienced by the learner as a form of social stratification where the teacher knows everything and the learner knows nothing (Ogle & Correa-Kovtun, 2010; Proctor, August, Carlo, & Snow, 2005; Szczepek, 2010; Wells, 2007).

9. *Be open to change*. There is no doubt that the demands of teaching in a multilingual classroom will require changes in those who teach there.

10. *Be reflective*. Good teachers reflect on their teaching practices and look for ways to improve them. In many ways you are an ambassador for English and all that it offers your learners. It is important to think about the effects you are having on your learners regardless of whether or not they are L1 or L2.

Phonemic Awareness

A high correlation exists between the ability to recognize spoken words as a sequence of individual sounds and reading achievement (Balmuth, 2009; Burke, Hagen-Burke, Kwok, & Parker, 2009; Cassady, Valadez, & Garrett, 2010; Kirk, 2001; Morag, 1999, 2004; Roskos, Tabors, & Lenhart, 2009). We have seen that explicit instruction can increase the phonemic awareness of children. To assist in determining the level of phonemic awareness in children, the following assessment items can be used.

Assessment 1: Isolation of beginning sounds. Ask the child what the first sounds of selected words are.

"What is the first sound of *dog*?"

Assessment 2: Deletion of initial sound. Read a word and ask the child to say it without the first sound.

"Say the word *cat*. Say *cat* without the /k/."

To begin, it is probably better to use words that will remain words when the first letter is eliminated.

Assessment 3: Segmentation of phonemes. Ask the child to say aloud the separate sounds of a word that is read.

"What are the two sounds in the word *go*?"

Assessment 4: Blending of phonemes. Slowly read the individual sounds of a word and ask the child to say what the word is.

"What word am I saying? /d/ /ô/ /g/."

Assessment 5: Phoneme manipulation. Read a word and ask the child to replace the initial sound with another. Have the child say the new word.

"In the word *fan*, the first sound is an /f/. If you replace the /f/ with an /m/, how would you say the new word?"

Letter Names

As discussed in Chapter 4, knowledge of letter names is not a prerequisite for learning to read. Although knowledge of letter names on entering school appears to be a predictor of later reading success, the relationship between knowing letter names and reading achievement is not one of cause and effect.

Based on a review of the research related to this issue, however, Groff (1984) states,

> At present, the following conclusion seems tenable: Letter name teaching is appropriate if done concurrently with instruction in phonics. Those who contend that the time of letter name teaching is unimportant probably are wrong.
>
> Since letter name knowledge and phonics knowledge are highly correlated, it makes sense to view them as functionally related areas of information. Thus, simultaneous teaching appears to be the best way to exploit their potential for helping children to learn to read. (p. 387)

Thus, it seems desirable at the beginning stages of reading instruction to assess children's knowledge of letter names. This information can be gleaned through assessments similar to those listed next.

Assessment 1: Develop flash cards for each letter of the alphabet, starting with lowercase. (Once lowercase letters are known, this exercise can be expanded to include uppercase letters.) In random order, present each card to the examinee and ask the student to name the letter. Record the examinee's responses on a scoring sheet. These data can be used to determine the appropriate letter name instruction for each child.

Assessment 2: Have the examinee write the letters of the alphabet as they are dictated in a random order. Analyze the results to determine which letters the examinee knows. Since the goal is letter name knowledge, either lower- or uppercase responses are correct. Responses that show the reverse (i.e., mirror image) form of a letter should also be considered correct.

Consonant Sounds

Several types of items can be used to determine if children understand the relationship between consonants and the letters that represent them. Most of the following examples offer ways of measuring recognition of the initial letter or letters of words (a) because of the essential role that this position plays in decoding words and (b) because this position is addressed first in instruction. However, the same kinds of assessments can be constructed for the endings of words as well.

Assessment 1: Letter to sound—single-consonant letters. Using flash cards of 19 single consonant letters (q and x do not have to be addressed at the beginning level), ask the child to say the sound represented by each. Record the child's responses.

Assessment 2: Letter to sound—single-consonant letters/pictures. Show the child a consonant letter followed by three pictures that name something. Ask the child to identify the picture whose name begins with the same sound as represented by the consonant letter. As examiner, name each picture slowly. Record the child's responses. The same 19 single-consonant letters as indicated in assessment 1 should be evaluated.

    m   [pictures of a]   (ball)   (moon)   (toy)

Assessment 3: Sound to letter—single-consonant letters. Provide the child with a score sheet that has four consonant letters after each item. For each, say a word and tell the child to circle the consonant letter that represents the first sound of the word.

toy   s   t   m   p

Assessment 4: Sound to letter—single-consonant letters. Have the child write the beginning letter of each word that you read. Vary words to include all 19 consonant letters mentioned in assessment 1.

Assessment 5: Letter to sound—consonant digraphs. Using flash cards of consonant digraphs (*th, ch, sh, wh*), ask the child to say the sound represented by each letter pair. Record the child's responses.

Assessment 6: Letter to sound—consonant digraphs/pictures. Show the child a consonant digraph followed by three pictures that name something. Ask the child to identify the picture whose name begins with the same sound as represented by the two letters. As examiner, name each picture slowly. Record the child's responses. The same four consonant digraphs as indicated in assessment 3 should be evaluated.

sh   [pictures of a]   (ship)   (church)   (sun)

Assessment 7: Sound to letters—consonant digraphs. Provide the child with a score sheet that has four consonant digraphs after each item. For each, say a word and tell the child to circle the consonant digraph that represents the first sound of the word.

chin   sh   th   ch   wh

Assessment 8: Sound to letters—consonant digraphs. Have the child write the first two letters of each word that you read. Vary the words so that they begin with *sh, th, ch,* and *wh.*

Assessment 9: Consonant letters representing blends. Using flash cards of letters representing several blends, ask the child to say the sound represented by each. Record the child's responses.

Assessment 10: Consonant letters representing blends/pictures. Show the child letters representing consonant blends followed by three pictures that name something. Ask the child to identify the picture whose name begins with the same sounds as represented by the consonant letters. As examiner, name each picture slowly. Record the child's responses.

tr   [pictures of a]   (top)   (train)   (thumb)

Assessment 11: Consonant letters representing blends—sound to letters. Provide the child with a score sheet that has letters representing four consonant blends after each item. For each, say a word and tell the child to circle the letters that represent the first sounds of the word.

blue   bl   st   br   fl

Assessment 12: Consonant letters representing blends—sound to letters. Have the child write the first two letters of each word you read. Vary the words to include several beginning blends.

Assessment 13: Consonant letters representing blends—phonograms. Construct words combining common phonograms (i.e., *an, ill, ig*) with letters representing blends. After reading and emphasizing the rime (the sound of a phonogram) part of the word family, ask the child to read the words of the family. Record the child's responses. Children may need the examiner to model this behavior for a couple of families.

an   bran   stan   blan   clan

Vowel Sounds

The following assessments measure children's knowledge about vowels.

Assessment 1:   Long and short vowels. Display flash cards of the five vowel letters (*a, e, i, o, u*) and ask the child to identify verbally the long sound and the short sound of each. Record the child's responses.

Assessment 2:   Short vowels. Read sets of three words, each containing the same medial vowel sound (short), and have the examinee write or verbally indicate what vowel sound the words contain. Vary sets to include all short vowel sounds.

pin   bit   him

Assessment 3:   Short vowels. Develop sets of five words (some will be nonsense words*) that vary only by a medial vowel. Have the child read each word list. Record the child's responses.

mat	pan	sap
met	pen	sep
mit	pin	sip
mot	pon	sop
mut	pun	sup

Assessment 4:   Long vowels. Read sets of three words, each containing the same medial vowel sound (long), and have the examinee write or indicate verbally what vowel sound the words contain. Vary sets to include all long vowel sounds.

site   night   hive

Assessment 5:   Long vowels (vowel–consonant–final *e* pattern). Develop sets of five words following the VCe pattern (some will be nonsense words), each

---

*When evaluating phonic skills with items that require the examinee to go from graphs to sounds, it is important to use words that are not part of the child's sight vocabulary. Therefore, this assessment and several that follow include nonsense words as a guard against obtaining misleading information.

with a different initial vowel letter. Have the child read each word list. Record the child's responses.

cake	pete	sime	rote	mute
gate	scene	mite	home	fuse
sate	pese	like	hoke	cube

Assessment 6: Short vowels (CVC) and long vowels (CVe). Develop a list of real-word and nonsense-word pairs that vary by a final *e*. Have the child read the word list and ask why she pronounced the words that way. Record the child's responses.

rote	rot
mit	mite
make	mak
set	sete
tune	tun

Assessment 7: Vowel digraphs. Develop a list of real words and nonsense words that contain the vowel digraphs (*ee, ea, ai, ay, oa*). Have the child read the word list. Record the child's responses.

keep	say
teap	mait
seat	seet
tay	boat
pain	soan

Assessment 8: Special digraphs. Develop a list of real words and nonsense words that contain special vowel digraphs (*oi, oy, ou, ow, oo, au*). Have the child read the word list. Record the child's responses.

soil	mou
koo	boy
out	poit
poy	cow
too	sook
dow	maul
good	paut

Assessment 9: r-controlled vowels. Develop a list of real words and nonsense words that contain r-controlled vowels. Have the child read the word list. Record the child's responses.

car	sert
purm	dare
turn	lar
sare	firm
term	kirn

CONCLUSION

It is not our intention to suggest that teachers should construct instruments that contain all the assessment items discussed in this chapter. The busy teacher may find excellent and useful resources in the form of ready-made assessments and other helpful tools in the extensive appendices of Shanker and Cockrum's *Locating and Correcting Reading Difficulites*, Ninth Edition, published by Allyn and Bacon. The representative assessment items included in the text should be considered as resource data from which teachers can pick and choose to assist in developing their own teacher-made assessment instruments. Finally, it should be restated at this point that the skills data that are collected from teacher-made and/or standardized tests should be verified or brought into question by observing and analyzing children as they attempt to use these skills in the act of reading.

CHAPTER 8: PRACTICE

1. Define what you believe diagnostic teaching to be.

   _____

   _____

   _____

   _____

   _____

   _____

2. To be effective, why is it necessary for teachers to become involved in diagnostic teaching?

   _____

   _____

   _____

   _____

3. Phonemic awareness, the ability to recognize spoken words as a sequence of individual sounds, shows a high correlation with reading achievement. Describe the following phoneme activities:

   a. Phoneme blending

   _____

   _____

_____

_____

_____

_____

b. Phoneme segmentation

_____

_____

_____

_____

_____

4. Discuss each of the following general principles of diagnosis as listed below:

a. Diagnosis should be viewed as a daily occurrence.

_____

_____

_____

_____

_____

b. Decisions about children should be based on diagnostic information collected from various sources.

_____

_____

_____

_____

_____

c. The identification of patterns of errors or miscues should be emphasized when analyzing diagnostic information.

_____

_____

_____

_____

_____

d. The focus should be on only one or two reading weaknesses at a time.

_____

_____

_____

_____

_____

e. Diagnosis for its own sake is not acceptable.

_____

_____

_____

f. What is the difference in emphasis between grapho-phonemic and syntactic–semantic approaches to beginning reading instruction?

_____

_____

_____

g. Why might a combination of a phonics approach and a meaning-centered approach be especially important in a multilingual classroom?

_____

_____

_____

_____

_____

h. What are several special roles that teachers in multilingual classrooms should play?

_____

_____

_____

CUMULATIVE REVIEW: CHAPTERS 1 TO 8

1. Define the following vocabulary before attempting the posttest in Chapter 9. If you encounter significant problems, go back to the text and review before continuing.

a. Phonics:

_____

_____

_____

b. Phonetics:

_____

_____

_____

c. Phoneme:

_____

_____

_____

d. Phonemic awareness:

_____

_____

_____

e. Consonant:

_____

_____

_____

f. Consonant blend:

_____

_____

_____

g. Vowel:

_____

_____

_____

h. Diphthong:

_____

_____

_____

i. R-controlled vowel:

_____

_____

_____

j. Schwa sound:

_____

_____

_____

k. Grapheme:

_____

_____

_____

l. Digraph:

_____

_____

_____

m. Onset:

_____

_____

_____

n. Rime:

_____

_____

_____

o. Phonogram:

_____

_____

_____

p. Syllable:

_____

_____

_____

q. Closed syllable:

_____

_____

_____

r. Open syllable:

_____

_____

_____

s. Breve:

_____

_____

_____

t. Circumflex:

_____

_____

_____

u. Macron:

_____

_____

_____

v. Umlaut:

_____

POINTS TO PONDER: AN INVITATION TO DIALOGUE

With another educator discuss the following questions:

1. What are some of the important ideas related to phonics that you have learned in the study of this text?

2. How will the application of your phonics knowledge change how you teach reading?

3. How will your diagnostic practices related to L2 learners change as result of this chapter?

4. If you had to identify a key teaching role identified in this chapter, which role do you feel is most critical to you and to the learners in your classroom?

FILL IN THE BLANKS

1. _____ is a method in which basic phonetics, the study of human speech sounds, is used to teach beginning reading.

2. A(n) _____ is placed over a vowel letter to show that it is pronounced as a long sound.

3. A(n) _____ is two letters that stand for a single phoneme.

4. A(n) _____ syllable ends with a consonant phoneme.

5. Sounds in a syllable represented by two or more letters that do not lose their own identity when blended together are known as _____ _____.

6. A(n) _____ is the smallest sound unit of a language that distinguishes one word from another.

7. A single vowel sound made of a blend of two vowel sounds in immediate sequence and pronounced in one syllable is known as a(n) _____ .

8. _____ , made up of a letter or combination of letters, represent phonemes.

9. A(n) _____ is a letter sequence comprised of a vowel grapheme and an ending consonant grapheme(s).

10. _____ are units of pronunciation consisting of a vowel alone or a vowel with one or more consonants.

11. _____ is the most common vowel sound in English.

12. _____ is the term used to describe pitch, stress, and intonation in linguistics.

13. The acronym TESOL stands for _____

14. The acronym DIBELS stands for _____

TRUE–FALSE

_____ 15. The irregularity of consonant sounds is a basic problem of phonics.

_____ 16. The schwa sound usually has a consistent spelling.

_____ 17. Phonics is _not_ the most important skill required for effective reading.

_____ 18. Almost any letter may, at some time, be silent.

_____ 19. A grapheme must be composed of one and only one letter.

_____ 20. Each syllable must contain only one vowel sound.

_____ 21. In attacking multisyllabic words, children must syllabicate before applying vowel generalizations.

_____ 22. There are over 200 ways to spell the 44 phonemes.

_____ 23. By the time the average child enters school, his or her auditory discrimination skills are fully developed.

_____ 24. The history of phonics shows that a phonics approach to teaching reading has been looked on favorably by most reading authorities over the past 50 years.

_____ 25. Language and identity are significant correlated.

_____ 26. Linguistic competence is the ability to use language appropriately in a cultural context.

_____ 27. Gestures and nonverbal communication should have no part in phonics instruction.

_____ 28. Music aids phonics learning.

_____ 29. Meaningful reading material aids phonics learning.

_____ 30. Reading diagnosis should be a continuous process in the classroom.

MULTIPLE CHOICE

_____ 31. Which of the following is a sound?
   a. consonant
   b. grapheme
   c. digraph
   d. None of the above

_____ 32. Which of the following words contains an open syllable?
   a. dove
   b. dog
   c. threw
   d. fire

_____ 33. Which of the following words contains a consonant digraph?

    a. blue

    b. string

    c. fly

    d. home

_____ 34. Which of the following words contains letters that represent a diphthong?

    a. show

    b. seat

    c. through

    d. out

_____ 35. How many phonemes are represented by the word _knight_?

    a. 2

    b. 3

    c. 4

    d. 5

_____ 36. How many phonemes are represented by the word _through_?

    a. 1

    b. 2

    c. 3

    d. 4

_____ 37. Which of the following pairs contains the same vowel phoneme?

    a. took—room

    b. grew—too

    c. food—wool

    d. None of the above

_____ 38. Which of the following letters do _not_ represent phonemes that are identified by their own name?

    a. c and s

    b. b and d

    c. y and x

    d. x and c

_____ 39. Which of the following consonant letters are most phonemically inconsistent in representing more than one sound?

    a. b and d

    b. c and g

    c. r and t

    d. m and p

_____ 40. Which of the following letter pairs represents a consonant blend?

    a. th

    b. fl

    c. zh

    d. wh

_____ 41. Which of the following nonsense words would most likely represent the "soft c" sound?
   a. cumb
   b. cimp
   c. cople
   d. calobe

_____ 42. Which of the following nonsense words would most likely represent the "hard g" sound?
   a. gilture
   b. weg
   c. gymp
   d. tuge

_____ 43. Which of the following consonant letters affects the vowel that precedes it?
   a. s
   b. t
   c. r
   d. None of the above

_____ 44. Which of the following words does _not_ contain a consonant blend?
   a. street
   b. chin
   c. brown
   d. fly

_____ 45. Which of the following words contains a closed syllable?
   a. grow
   b. why
   c. boy
   d. rote

Circle the item in each list that does not belong. Explain your reason for each choice.

46. phoneme   digraph   diphthong   vowel

_____

47. th   tw   ch   ng   wh

_____

48. got   home   low   boy   high

_____

49. boy   pout   ounce   toil   double

_____

50. cuple   capon   cepp   cobat

_____

How many phonemes are represented in the following words? Write each word using its phoneme pronunciation symbols.

51. blue   _____   _____

52. herd   _____   _____

53. toxic   _____   _____

54. should   _____   _____

55. who   _____   _____

56. air   _____   _____

57. quit   _____   _____

58. antique   _____   _____

59. said   _____   _____

60. school   _____   _____

The following questions should be answered by using the vowel generalizations that are often taught in elementary schools. Each question requires the vowel pronunciation contained in a nonsense word.

_____ 61. The *i* in *dif* has the same sound as:

    a. girl.

    b. in.

    c. sight.

    d. None of the above.

_____ 62. The *u* in *smupe* has the same sound as:

    a. hurt.

    b. pup.

    c. use.

    d. None of the above.

_____ 63. The *a* in *kna* has the same sound as:

    a. mart.

    b. ate.

    c. map.

    d. None of the above.

_____ 64. The *e* in *reab* has the same sound as:

    a. bee.

    b. err.

    c. send.

    d. None of the above.

_____ 65. The *i* in *lirp* has the same sound as:

    a. bin.

    b. high.

    c. whirl.

    d. None of the above.

_____ 66. The *u* in *nupp* has the same sound as:

    a. hurt.

    b. cup.

    c. prude.

    d. None of the above.

_____ 67. The first *e* in *zeet* has the same sound as:

    a. me.

    b. err.

    c. send.

    d. None of the above.

_____ 68. The *u* in *tue* has the same sound as:

    a. cup.

    b. hurt.

    c. use.

    d. None of the above.

Indicate where the syllabic divisions occur in the following vowel-consonant letter patterns, nonsense words, or real words. Knowledge of syllabication generalizations is essential. There are no consonant digraphs in questions 69 to 72 (C = consonant letter, V = vowel letter).

_____ 69. CVCVCC

    a. CV-CV-CC

    b. CVC-VCC

    c. CV-CVCC

    d. CVCV-CC

_____ 70. CVCCVC

    a. CV-CCVC

    b. CVCC-VC

    c. CVC-CVC

    d. CV-CC-VC

_____ 71. VCCVC

    a. VC-CVC

    b. V-CCVC

    c. VCC-VC

    d. VCCVC

_____ 72. CCVCVCC

    a. CCVC-VCC

    b. CCV-C-VCC

    c. CC-VC-VCC

    d. CCV-CVCC

_____ 73. ralagasins

    a. ra-la-ga-sins

    b. ral-a-ga-sins

     c. ral-ag-a-sins
     d. ra-la-gas-ins

_____ 74. soctaluca

     a. soc-ta-lu-ca
     b. soc-tal-u-ca
     c. soct-al-u-ca
     d. soct-a-lu-ca

_____ 75. plukle

     a. pluk-le
     b. plukle
     c. pl-u-kle
     d. plu-kle

_____ 76. exanphema

     a. exan-phe-ma
     b. ex-an-phe-ma
     c. ex-an-phem-a
     d. e-xan-phe-ma

_____ 77. megmer

     a. me-gmer
     b. meg-mer
     c. megm-er
     d. megmer

Reading programs often introduce long and short vowel sounds based on spelling patterns. In the following patterns (V = vowel letter; C = consonant letter), indicate which vowel sound you would expect the pattern to represent (L = long sound; S = short sound).

_____ 78. VC
_____ 79. VCe (_e_ = final _e_ in word)
_____ 80. CVCC
_____ 81. CV

MATCHING

For each of the numbered items in column A, write the letter from column A that best matches the item's meaning.

Column A	_Column B_
_____ 82. The LEAR	a. The most common cause of reading failure
_____ 83. Two common intrusive letters	b. A brief form of reading assessment

_____ 84. Guiding

_____ 85. Running record

_____ 86. Vision

_____ 87. Miscue

_____ 88. Critical Age Hypothesis

_____ 89. Semantic–syntactic approach

_____ 90. Grapho-phonemic approach

c. A synthetic reading method

d. A misapplication of psycholinguistic cues

e. Meaning-centered reading instruction

f. Optimal time to learn language

g. Dictated reading material

h. L and R

i. Scaffolding

A Appendix
Answer Key

CHAPTER 1: PRACTICE

1. is not
2. second
3. contextual, structural
4. letters, sounds
5. synthetic
6. Analytic
7. Developing linguistic competence early in the learning experience of bilingual learners provides essential scaffolding for further learning and the confidence to learn it.
8. Answers will vary.
9. In learning phonics, children must have the opportunity to see, hear, and say the components they are being asked to learn. Initial instruction and practice in phonics should concentrate, therefore, on oral activities.
10. The purpose of phonics is to assist children in systematically decoding words that are unknown to them by teaching them the relationships between letters and speech sounds. Phonics for the sake of phonics should never be the goal of instruction.
11. Systematic synthetic phonics instruction has a positive effect on reading skills. The advantages of asking students to articulate phonemes in isolation outweigh the disadvantages.

CHAPTER 2: PHONICS PRETEST

1. b
2. f
3. h
4. e
5. a
6. d

7. j

8. i

9. c

10. g

11. True

12. False

13. False

14. True

15. True

16. False

17. True

18. False

19. False

20. False

21. True

22. True

23. True

24. False

25. True

26. b

27. c

28. b

29. d

30. c

31. c

32. b

33. d

34. b

35. b

36. a

37. b

38. c

39. b

40. b

41. *th* is a consonant digraph, and the others are letters that represent consonant blends.

42. *st* represents a consonant blend, while the others are consonant digraphs.

43. *s* is the only letter that does not, at some time, represent a vowel sound.

44. *low* is the only word that does not contain letters representing the diphthong sound.

45. *gym* is the only word that contains a "soft g."

46. b

47. c

48. c

49. b

50. b

51. d

52. b

53. c

54. b

55. c

56. a

57. d

58. b

59. a

60. d

61. b

62. b

63. S

64. L

65. S

66. L

67. a. Mentor,

b. Translator,

c. Guide. (Order will vary)

68. Answers will vary, but since cultural identity and language are intertwined, reference should be made in the response to aspects of the following:

a. Different cultures respond differently to the process of instruction.

b. In some cultures, the gender of the teacher matters. Females, for example, should not be instructed by male teachers in some Asian and other cultures.

c. Not all languages stem from an alphabetic system, making the transition to English difficult.

69. Answers will vary, but since teacher reflection and self-assessment should be integral to the process of teaching to begin with, a composite of some of the following concepts should appear in your response:

a. *Tolerance* toward indidividual differences in your classroom is imperative. This includes linguistic differences as well as learning differences.

b. *Patience* is necessary with struggling learners who do not come from learning-ready backgrounds, either linguistically or otherwise.

c. *Preparedness* and *flexibility* in lesson design and application and the willingness to reflect on and change aspects of your teaching style will help accommodate best practices in phonics instruction.

70. Answers will vary.

CHAPTER 2: PRACTICE

Answers will vary.

CUMULATIVE REVIEW: CHAPTERS 1 AND 2

1. contextual analysis, structural analysis
2. is not
3. are
4. outweigh
5. has not
6. synthetic
7. As children build larger sight vocabularies, they appear to rely less on phonics in many cases and more on the power of analogy, comparing unknown words to words that are known. Once children build this storehouse of words and progress beyond the beginning levels of reading, such elements as background knowledge, vocabulary, and general ability to reason become significantly more important in comprehending text.
8. *Explicit* or synthetic phonics emphasizes the learning of individual sounds, often in isolation, and follows with instruction that teaches children how to blend these individual sounds to form words (a part-to-whole approach). *Implicit* or analytic phonics, on the other hand, begins with whole words and identifies individual sounds as parts of those words. Efforts are made to avoid pronouncing letter sounds in isolation (a whole-to-part approach).
9. The whole language philosophy is certainly compatible with the teaching of phonics. Because of its emphasis on a whole-to-part approach, it would tend to emphasize implicit or analytic phonics.
10. Although the reader may pronounce an unknown word correctly, if it is not part of her speaking–listening vocabulary, she would have no way of knowing whether she was correct.

CHAPTER 3: PRACTICE

1. phoneme, vowel, rime, diphthong, consonant
2. a, e, i, o, u, y, w

3. go, dew, through

4. digraph

5. bri<u>ng</u>, <u>th</u>e, <u>sh</u>ut, <u>ch</u>ill

6. d<u>ew</u>, l<u>oo</u>k, s<u>ou</u>p, b<u>oy</u>, b<u>ea</u>t

7. diphthong, /ou/

8. sound

9. macron

10. breve

11. digraph

12. closed

13. digraph

14. phonetics

15. 44, 25, 19

16. inconsistent

17. vowel sounds

18. too—shoes

19. a.   coil   /oi/

    b.   out   /ou/

    d.   owl   /ou/

20. *c, q, x*

21. /s/   /zh/

    /k/   /f/

    /n/   /j/

    /sh/   /h/

    /ng/   /g/

    /hw/   /k/

22. /ā/   /û/

    /ī/   /ă/

    /oi/   /ou/

    /ū/   /ŏo/

    /ŏ/   /ě/

    /ooo/   /ŭ/

23. 2, /s/ /ō/

    3, /s/ /ĭ/ /ng/

    3, /b/ /l/ /oo/

4, /g/ /ō/ /s/ /t/

3, /sh/ /ĭ/ /p/

3, /ō/ /l/ /d/

2, /b/ /oi/

4, /b/ /û/ /r/ /d/

3, /b/ /ō/ /th/

4, /b/ /ŏ/ /k/ /s/

4, /s/ /ĕ/ /n/ /t/

3, /k/ /ō/ /m/

2, /k/ /ou/

2, /l/ /ō/

24. *Vowel:* sounds represented by *a, e, i, o, u,* and sometimes *y* and *w.*

Grapheme: a letter or combination of letters that represnts a phoneme.

Phoneme: the smallest sound unit of a language that distinguishes one word from another.

Consonant: sounds represented by any letter of the English alphabet except *a, e, i, o,* and *u.*

Syllable: a unit of pronunciation that consists of a vowel alone or a vowel with one or more consonants. There is only one vowel phoneme in each syllable.

Macron: the orthographic symbol (ˉ) placed over a vowel letter to show that it is pronounced as a long sound.

Open syllable: any syllable that ends with a vowel phoneme.

Breve: the orthographic symbol (ˆ) placed over a vowel letter to show that it is pronounced as a short sound.

Digraph: two letters that stand for a single phoneme.

Rime: the part of a syllable that includes the vowel sound and any consonant sound(s) following it.

CUMULATIVE REVIEW: CHAPTERS 1 TO 3

1. are

2. has

3. blend, street

4. Answers will vary. (Example: few)

5. Synthetic

6. Analytic

7. Phonics helps only if the unknown word is part of the reader's speaking-listening vocabulary.

8. whole-word. *Pneumonia* does not follow many phonic generalizations, especially vowel generalizations. Consequently, efforts spent with a whole-word emphasis would most likely produce better results.

9. A *digraph* is two *letters* that stand for a single phoneme, while a *diphthong* is a single vowel *sound* made up of a glide from one vowel to another. For example, in the word *oil*, the letters *oi* form the digraph, while the sound /oi/ is the diphthong.

10. A consonant digraph is two *letters* that stand for a single sound. A consonant blend is a combination of *sounds* in a syllable represented by two or more letters that are blended together without losing their own identities.

11. A phonogram is a letter sequence composed of a vowel grapheme and an ending consonant grapheme(s). A rime is the sound a phonogram represents.

12. The *r* renders the vowel neither long nor short. (Examples: st<u>a</u>r, d<u>a</u>re, h<u>e</u>r, f<u>o</u>r)

13. Learning letter–sound associations enables children to apply this knowledge in the process of decoding unknown words.

14. The syllable *is* the basic unit of pronunciation in English.

15. Answers will vary, but they should reflect the fact that transition from one alphabetic system to another is facilitated greatly by knowledge of the L1 or first language alphabet, making learning of the second or L2 language much more efficient.

CHAPTER 4: PRACTICE

1. is

2. Oral language serves as an essential foundation on which reading instruction can and should be built.

3. Phonemic awareness

4. segmentation

5. blending

6. In instruction the focus on one or two skills produces greater transfer than a multiskilled approach. Phoneme segmentation and blending are basic and belong in beginning instructional programs.

7. There is no cause-and-effect relationship between knowledge of ABCs and effective reading. This knowledge is simply indicative of a host of factors that are often conducive to learning to read.

8. Reading is a visual act that requires effective near-point (close) vision. Yet the types of tests often administered to children at the beginning stages of schooling simply measure far-point (distant) vision.

9. is not

10. Teachers need to realize that the wide range of experiences that children have had with language before formal schooling begins should be used in assisting them to learn to read. Children's understanding about print awareness, concepts of print, sense of story, oral language, and writing will have a significant bearing on their ultimate success in reading achievement.

CUMULATIVE REVIEW: CHAPTERS 1 TO 4

1. rime
2. diphthong
3. rime
4. open
5. consonant blend
6. schwa
7. breve
8. diphthong
9. True
10. False
11. No. Phonics should be viewed as a means to an end.
12. *Phoneme:* the smallest unit of a language that distinguishes one word from another.
    Grapheme: a letter or combination of letters that represents a phoneme.
    Digraph: two letters that stand for a single phoneme.
    Onset: the consonant sound(s) of a syllable that come(s) before the vowel sound.
13. Phonics
14. consonant phoneme
15. grapheme
16. False
17. syllable
18. schwa
19. Answers will vary.
20. st<u>ew</u>, <u>the</u>, <u>why</u>, star, m<u>ee</u>t, <u>sh</u>ut, glove, g<u>oo</u>d, si<u>ng</u>, glut
21. b<u>oy</u>, could, <u>owl</u>, <u>out</u>, p<u>oi</u>nt, c<u>ow</u>, b<u>oi</u>l, own, c<u>oi</u>n, t<u>ow</u>n
22. /k/   /ng/
    /hw/   /f/
    /zh/   /h/
    /k/ /s/   /k/
    /k/ /w/   /j/

23. /â/   /ô/
    /ä/   /ä/
    /ô/   /û/
    /ooo/ /oˆo
    /ou/   /û/

24. 2, /ô/ /f/
    5, /f/ /ū/ /ch/ /û/ /r/
    5, /n/ /ā/ /k/ /ĭ/ /d/
    3, /t/ /r/ /oo/
    4, /p/ /l/ /oo/ /m/
    4, /f/ /ˇu/ /n/ /ē/
    4, /k/ /w/ /ē/ /n/
    4, /m/ /ĭ/ /k/ /s/
    3, /h/ /â/ /r/

CHAPTER 5: PRACTICE

1. consonant, vowel
2. cint, cymp, sluce
3. /ch/, /k/, /sh/
4. only one, is
5. Inductive
6. gultion, seg
7. silent
8. consonant digraph, /k/
9. c
10. a
11. c
12. a
13. b
14. d
15. c
16. b
17. it is not the final letter.
18. it is the final letter.
19. long, silent
20. long, silent

CUMULATIVE REVIEW: CHAPTERS 1 TO 5

1. False

2. phonetics

3. macron

4. vowel

5. smallest

6. digraph

7. Auditory discrimination

8. is not. It is quite possible that a child will be ready to learn under one set of instructional conditions and not be ready to learn under another.

9. /aˇ/   /ô/

   /uˇ/   / /

   /oˆo   /ĕ/

   /ĭ/   /û/

10. /j/   /hw/

    /g/   /f/

    /k/   /k/ /s/

    /h/   /s/

11. 3, /f/ /ō/ /n/

    2, /ou/ /t/

    2, /n/ /oo/

    4, / / /b/ /ou/ /t/

    3, /ô/ /t/ /ō/

    3, /k/ /oˇo/ /d/

    2, /t/ /oi/

    4, /p/ /û/ /r/ /l/

    5, /p/ /oˇo/ /d/ /ĭ/ /ng/

    3, /d/ /â/ /r/

12. near-point

13. Auditory acuity

14. False. The relationship is not one of cause and effect. Knowledge of letter names does not cause one to become a better reader.

15. Visual discrimination must be done with letters and/or words. Practice with geometric figures and pictures does not transfer to the type of visual discrimination needed for reading.

CHAPTER 6: PRACTICE

1. vowel sounds

2. 19

3. schwa

4. is not

5. (Answer for words will vary.)

c	/s/, /k/
g	/g/, /j/
s	/s/, /z/
x	/z/
	/k/ /s/
	/g/ /z/

6. /s/

    /k/

    /j/

    /g/

7. consonant blends

8.
B	B	D	B
D	D	B	B
B	D	B	D
D	B	D	B
D	B	B	B

9.
CVC	short
CV	long
Vce	long
VC	short

10. Vowel sounds are far more stable within particular phonograms than they are in isolation.

11. Current research suggests that the critical age for language learning spans the elementary and early middle school years. To have the greatest potential impact on either bilingual or first language learning, it is important to focus appropriate resources where they are likely to be most effective, which is in the elementary and early middle school years for the learner.

12. Delaying instruction for either first language or bilingual learners, in the case of L2 children, misses opportunites for language learning that are unique to this period of development.

13. Consonants
14. The schwa sound, or simply schwa.
15. The same.
16. l and r
17. gradually

CUMULATIVE REVIEW: CHAPTERS 1 TO 6

1. does not appear
2. second
3. *Phonics:* A method in which basic phonetics is used to teach reading.

   Phoneme: The smallest sound unit of a language that distinguishes one word from another.

   Open syllable: Any syllable that ends with a vowel phoneme.

   Macron: The symbol (–) placed over a vowel letter to show it is pronounced as a long sound.

   Consonant: A sound represented by any letter of the English alphabet except *a, e, i, o, u.*

   Digraph: Two letters that stand for a single phoneme (sound).

   Syllable: A unit of pronunciation consisting of a vowel alone or a vowel with one or more consonants. There is only one vowel phoneme in each syllable.
4. <u>ou</u>t, b<u>oo</u>k, <u>th</u>at

   so<u>ng</u>, <u>ch</u>at, <u>kn</u>ob
5. grapheme
6. /k/   /k/ /w/

   /h/   /k/ /s/

   silent   /s/

   /zh/   /k/
7. /â/   /ō/

   /ə/   /ô/

   /ŏ/   /ou/

   /û/   /o͝o/
8. 3, /r/ /ĕ/ /d/

   3, /k/ /ō/ /t/

   3, /hw/ /ē/ /l/

   4, /k/ /w/ /ĭ/ /t/

   2, /h/ /oo/

3, /hw/ /ĕ/ /n/
3, /f/ /l/ /ī/
4, /k/ /û/ /r/ /s/
7, /d/ /ī/ / / /l/ /ĕ/ /k/ /t/

9. "Emergent literacy is concerned with the earliest phases of literacy development, the period between birth and the time when children read and write conventionally. The term *emergent literacy* signals a belief that, in a literate society, young children—even one- and two-year olds— are in the process of becoming literate" (Sulzby & Teale, 1991, p. 728). Thus, if young children have had little opportunity to experiment with reading and writing before they enter school, it can have a significant negative impact on their achievement.

10. Answers will vary. However, the fact that the relationship is not one of cause and effect should be included in the answer. Knowledge of letter names does not cause one to become a better reader.

11. *Coat:* When two successive vowel letters occur in a syllable and they are not any of the special digraphs (oi, oy, ow, ou, oo, au), the first is usually long and the second is silent (especially ee—keep, ea—meat, ai—pain, ay—say, oa—load).

    Hope: When two vowel letters in a syllable are separated by a consonant and one is a final *e*, the first usually records its long sound, and the *e* is silent.

    She: A single vowel letter in a syllable usually represents the long sound if it is the final letter.

    But: A single vowel letter in a syllable usually represents the short sound if it is not the final letter.

12. The term *generalizations* better represents the fact that there are exceptions to the letter–sound associations we teach children.

CHAPTER 7: PRACTICE

1. first
2. vowel
3. are
4. d, t
5. silent
6. are not
7. one
8. between the consonants.
9. Although double consonant letters are generally separated when words are broken into syllables in writing, the sound will be represented in only one syllable.

10. *Vowel-Consonant Letter Patterns*

V-CV	#9
VC-CV	#8
V-CVC	#9
CVC-CV	#8
CCVC-CVC	#8
CCV-CVC	#9
VCe	No division, as final <u>e</u> is silent

Real Words

a-mass	#9
a-phis	#6, #9
bel-dam	#8
re-ta-ble	#2, #4
bo-lide	#9
cu-pule	#9
foxed	#2b
fur-be-low	#5, #8, #9
ju-di-ca-ture	#2a, #9

Nonsense Words

pre-an-the-ma	#2, #6, #8, #9
un-bot-ed	#2, #2b
e-ma-kle	#4, #9
e-pe-ture	#2a, #9
gra-peet	#5, #9
re-sired	#2, #2b
e-cad	#9
an-tole	#8
scrnt	no vowel letter, no vowel sound, no word
ma-shot	#6, #9
haulm	#5
sub-ton-en	#2

CUMULATIVE REVIEW: CHAPTERS 1 TO 7

1. are
2. outweigh
3. grapheme, digraph, phonogram
4. *y, w*
5. gone, dove, tire
6. ri<u>ng</u>, <u>th</u>at, <u>sh</u>ucks, <u>ch</u>ain
7. <u>few</u>, g<u>oo</u>d, f<u>ee</u>t, <u>oi</u>l, s<u>ou</u>p
8. segmentation
9. rime
10. diphthong
11. 44, 25, 19
12. too, room, shoes
13. *c, q, x*
14. it is not the last letter
15. long, silent
16. /ă/   /zh/

    /â/   /ng/

    /ī/   /k/

    /oi/   /g/

17. Reading is a visual act that requires effective near-point vision. Yet the types of tests often administered to children at the beginning stages of school measure only far-point vision.

18. Research has shown that a positive relationship exists between oral language and reading achievement. Oral language appears to serve as an essential foundation on which reading instruction can and should be built.

19. Segmentation is the process of isolating all the sounds of a word, while blending is the process of recognizing isolated speech sounds and the ability to pronounce the word for which they stand. (Examples will vary.)

20. No. To be effective, phonics instruction must be oral in nature. Children need to hear and speak the language to get the full benefit of instruction.

21. The synthetic approach generally emphasizes the learning of individual sounds, often in isolation, and follows with instruction that teaches children how to blend these individual sounds to form words (a part-to-whole approach). The analytic approach, on the other hand, begins with whole words and identifies individual sounds as part of those words. Efforts are made to avoid pronouncing letter sounds in isolation (a whole-to-part approach).

22. Consonants are more consistent in their spelling than are vowel sounds. Written English has a left-to-right orientation whereby the initial position of words assumes the most significant position in word recognition. Most of the words that children are initially asked to learn begin with consonant sounds.

23. Answers will vary.

24. As children begin to work with an increasing number of unknown polysyllabic words, they must be able to syllabicate them correctly first before applying vowel generalizations.

25. *Phonetics:* The scientific study of human speech sounds.

    Grapheme: A letter or combination of letters that represents a phoneme.

    Vowels: Sounds represented by *a, e, i, o, u,* and sometimes *y* and *w.*

    Diphthong: A single vowel sound made up of a glide from one vowel to another in immediate sequence and pronounced in one syllable.

    Consonant blend: Sounds in a syllable represented by two or more letters that are blended together without losing their own identities.

    Rime: The part of a syllable that includes the vowel sound and any consonant sound(s) that come(s) after it.

    Schwa: An unstressed sound commonly occurring in unstressed syllables. It closely resembles the sound of a short *u.*

CHAPTER 8: PRACTICE

1. Diagnostic teaching is the process whereby teachers identify students' strengths and weaknesses through both formal and informal means and use this diagnostic information to direct their instructional actions.

2. Unless teachers have diagnostic information to assist in the identification of the strengths and weaknesses of students, it is extremely difficult to set up instructional programs that allow students the opportunity to grow to their full potential.

3. a. Phoneme blending is the process of recognizing isolated speech sounds and the ability to pronounce the word for which they stand when combined.

   b. Phoneme segmentation is the ability to isolate all the sounds of a word.

4. a. Diagnosis should be viewed as a daily occurrence. Diagnosis is too often treated as a special event that takes place only once or twice a year. In reality, teachers need to observe and evaluate children on a continuing basis because children's needs and/or skills can change drastically over a short period.

   b. Decisions about children should be based on diagnostic information collected from various sources. Instructional decisions about children should never be made on the basis of a single test or observation. Generally, the more diverse the data that teachers collect, the more useful the information.

c. The identification of patterns of error should be emphasized when analyzing diagnostic information. If a type of error occurs in a pattern, greater confidence can be placed on the interpretation that the error is truly a problem for the child. When decisions are based on isolated errors, unneeded instruction and practice often follow.

d. The focus should be on only one or two reading weaknesses at a time. Often, when diagnosing children who exhibit problems in reading, several weaknesses will be identified. If attempts are made to remediate all these weaknesses at once, it generally overwhelms the children and further frustrates their efforts to improve. Narrow the skills to be taught to the one or two that appear to create the most difficulty and remediate these before continuing with others that are less debilitating.

e. Diagnosis for its own sake is not acceptable; it must lead to specific instructional action. Teachers must avoid becoming so enamored of the diagnostic process that they lose sight of the ultimate objective of diagnosis: the identification and remediation of weaknesses or disabilities.

f. What is the difference in emphasis between grapho-phonemic and syntactic–semantic approaches to beginning reading instruction? The grapho-phonemic approach centers its attention on the sound–symbol relationship between the phonemes of English and the graphemes or symbols that represent these sounds. In the syntactic–semantic approach the focus is more on the meaningful relationship between the order of words and their semantic properties. This text focuses on the relationship between phonemes and the graphemes that represent them.

g. Why might a combination of a phonics approach and a meaning-centered approach be especially important in a multilingual classroom? All children benefit when meaning is embedded within their reading material. This is especially important if the L2 learner does not have a strong base in English vocabulary.

h. Any of the 10 roles may satisfy this answer.

CUMULATIVE REVIEW: CHAPTERS 1 TO 8

a. Phonics: A method in which basic phonetics, the study of human speech sounds, is used to teach beginning reading. Teachers teach phonics, not phonetics.

b. Phonetics: The study of human speech sounds.

c. Phoneme: The smallest *sound* unit of a language that distinguishes one word from another. Examples: the phoneme /h/ distinguishes *hat* from *at*; the words *tell* and *yell* are distinguished by their initial phonemes /t/ and /y/. (This text indicates that there are 44 phonemes in the American-English language. This number varies, however, according to different authorities and/or dialects. Slash marks, //, are used throughout the text to indicate that the reference is to a *sound* and not a *letter*.)

d. Phonemic awareness: The ability to recognize spoken words as a sequence of individual sounds.

e. Consonant: A sound represented by any letter of the English alphabet except *a, e, i, o, u*. Consonants are sounds made by closing or restricting the breath channel.

f. Consonant blend: Sounds in a syllable represented by two or more letters that are blended together without losing their own identities. Examples: blue /b/ /l/; gray /g/ /r/; brown /b/ /r/; twig /t/ /w/; street /s/ /t/ /r/; flip /f/ /l/.

g. Vowel: A sound represented by *a, e, i, o, u*, and sometimes *y* and *w*, in the English alphabet. Vowels are sounds made without closing or restricting the breath channel.

h. Diphthong: A single vowel sound made up of a glide from one vowel sound to another in immediate sequence and pronounced in one syllable. Examples: /oi/ in oil and boy; /ou/ in house and owl. (Phonetics would consider that some single-letter vowels represent diphthongs. For the purposes of teaching reading, however, only /oi/ and /ou/ will be considered diphthongs.)

i. R-controlled vowel: When a vowel letter is followed by the letter *r*, it affects the vowel sound so that it is neither short nor long. For example, in *her*, the vowel sound becomes /û/; in *dare*, it becomes /â/; in *for*, it becomes /ô/; in *car*, it becomes /ä/.

j. Schwa sound: An unstressed sound commonly occurring in unstressed syllables. It is represented by the symbol /ə/ and closely resembles the short sound for *u*. Examples: *a* in *about; o* in *occur; i* in *pencil; u* in *circus*.

k. Grapheme: A letter or combination of letters that represents a phoneme (sound). Examples: the phoneme /b/ in *bat* is represented by the grapheme *b;* the phoneme /f/ in *phone* is represented by the grapheme *ph*. (There are over 200 different ways to spell the phonemes. For example, /f/ can take the form of *f* in *fine, gh* in *cough,* and *ph* in *elephant*. This is an example of three different graphemes representing the same phoneme.)

l. Digraph: Two letters that stand for a single phoneme (sound). Examples: thin /th/; each /ĕ/; shop /sh/; boy /oi/; look /ŏo/; rang /ng/; few /oo/. A digraph is simply a grapheme of two letters.

m. Onset: The consonant sound(s) of a syllable that comes before the vowel sound. (Examples are included with the definition of *rime* below.)

n. Rime: The part of a syllable that includes the vowel sound and any consonant sound(s) that come(s) after it. The graphic representation of a rime is referred to as a *phonogram*. Following are examples of both onsets and rimes.

Word	Onset	Rime	Phonogram
mat	/m/	/at/	at
pig	/p/	/ig/	ig
at	—	/at/	at
split	/spl/	/it/	it

o. Phonogram: A letter sequence comprised of a vowel grapheme and an ending consonant grapheme(s), such as *-ig* in *wig, dig, big,* or the *-ack* in *back, tack, sack.* From phonograms we can generate word families.

p. Syllable: A unit of pronunciation consisting of a vowel alone or a vowel with one or more consonants. There can be only one vowel phoneme (sound) in each syllable.

q. Closed syllable: Any syllable that ends with a consonant phoneme (sound). Examples: come /m/; paste /t/; love /v/; ran /n/.

r. Open syllable: Any syllable that ends with a vowel sound (phoneme). Examples: see /ē/; may /ā/; boy /oi/; auto /ō/.

s. Breve: The orthographic symbol (ˆ) placed over a vowel letter to show it is pronounced as a short sound (sometimes called an unglided vowel).

t. Circumflex: The orthographic symbol (ˆ) placed above vowel graphemes to indicate pronunciation.

u. Macron: The orthographic symbol (¯) placed over a vowel letter to show it is pronounced as a long sound (sometimes called a glided vowel).

v. Umlaut: The orthographic symbol (¨) placed above vowel graphemes to indicate pronunciation.

CHAPTER 9: PHONICS POST-TEST

1. Phonics
2. macron
3. digraph
4. closed
5. consonant blends
6. phoneme
7. diphthong
8. Graphemes
9. phonogram
10. Syllables
11. schwa
12. supersegmentals
13. Teaching English to second language learners
14. Dynamic Indicators of Basic Early Literacy Skills
15. False
16. False
17. True
18. True

19. False

20. True

21. True

22. True

23. False

24. False

25. True

26. True

27. False

28. True

29. True

30. True

31. a

32. c

33. b

34. d

35. b

36. c

37. b

38. d

39. b

40. b

41. b

42. b

43. c

44. b

45. d

46. *digraph* refers to letters; the other terms refer to sounds.

47. *tw* represents a consonant blend; the others are consonant digraphs.

48. *boy* is the only word that contains letters that represent the diphthong sound.

49. *double* is the only word that does not contain letters representing the diphthong sound.

50. *cepp* is the only word that contains a "soft c."

51. 3,/b/ /l/ /oo/

52. 4,/h/ /û/ /r/ /d/

53. 6,/t/ /ŏ/ /k/ /s/ /ĭ/ /k/

54. 3,/sh/ /ŏo/ /d/
55. 2,/sh/ /oo/
56. 2,/â/ /r/
57. 4,/k/ /w/ /ĭ/ /t/
58. 5,/ă/ /n/ /t/ /ē/ /k/
59. 3,/s/ /ĕ/ /d/
60. 4,/s/ /k/ /oo/ /l/
61. b
62. c
63. b
64. a
65. c
66. b
67. a
68. c
69. c
70. c
71. a
72. d
73. a
74. a
75. d
76. b
77. b
78. S
79. L
80. S
81. L
Matching
82. g
83. h
84. i
85. b
86. a
87. d
88. f
89. e
90. c

Glossary

accent (primary): The syllable in a word that receives the strongest and loudest emphasis.

allophone: A sound variant of a single phoneme that may be indistinguishable to speakers of another language. Example: /l/ and /r/.

analytic phonics: A whole-to-part phonics approach that emphasizes starting with whole words and identifying individual sounds as parts of those words. Efforts are generally made to avoid pronouncing letter sounds in isolation; also known as *implicit phonics*.

approximates: In linguistics, a classification category often describing the sounds /l/ and /r/.

auditory discrimination: The ability to hear similarities and differences between sounds as they occur in spoken words.

base word: A word to which prefixes and/or suffixes are added to create new but related words. The simplest member of a word family.

breve: An orthographic diacritic symbol (˘) placed above vowel graphemes to indicate pronunciation. Please see: www.merriam-webster.com/help/pronguide.htm for a complete list with examples of English diacritics along with examples and their pronunciation.

circumflex: An orthographic diacritic symbol (ˆ) placed above vowel graphemes to indicate pronunciation.

closed syllable: Any syllable ending with a consonant phoneme. Examples: come /m/; love /v/; ran /n/.

compound word: A word made up of two or more base words.

consonant blend: Sounds in a syllable represented by two or more letters that are blended together without losing their identity. Examples: blue /b/ /l/; brown /b/ /r/; twig /t/ /w/; street /s/ /t/ /r/; flip /f/ /l/.

consonants: Sounds represented by any letter of the English alphabet except *a, e, i, o,* and *u*. Consonants are *sounds* that are made by closing or restricting the breath channel.

decoding: The process of determining the pronunciation of an unknown word.

deductive instruction: Instructional procedure that centers on telling children about generalizations and having them apply the generalizations to specific words; a general-to-specific emphasis.

diacritic: Special symbol used above vowel letters to indicate their pronunciation.

dialect: A phonological, semantic, and grammatical variant of a language.

DIBELS: Dynamic Indicators of Basic Early Literacy Skills -a set of measures and procedures that evaluate the foundational skills of reading including phonemic awareness, alphabetic knowledge, accuracy and fluency, reading comprehension and vocabulary.

digraph: Two letters that stand for a single phoneme. Examples: <u>th</u>in /th/; each /ē/; <u>sh</u>op /sh/; b<u>oy</u> /oi/; l<u>oo</u>k /o͞o/; ra<u>ng</u> /ng/; f<u>ew</u> /oo/. A digraph is simply a grapheme of two letters.

diphthong: A single vowel sound made up of a blend of two vowel sounds in immediate sequence and pronounced in one syllable. Examples: /oi/ in <u>oi</u>l and b<u>oy</u>; /ou/ in h<u>ou</u>se and <u>ow</u>l. (Phonetics would classify some single-letter vowels as diphthongs. For the purposes of teaching reading, however, only /oi/ and /ou/ are considered diphthongs.)

ESL: English as a Second Language.

grapheme: A letter or combination of letters that represents a phoneme. Examples: the phoneme /b/ in *bat* is represented by the grapheme *b*; the phoneme /f/ in *phone* is represented by the grapheme *ph*. There are over 200 different ways to spell the phonemes. For example, /f/ can take the form of *f* in *fine, gh* in *cough,* and *ph* in *elephant,* three different graphemes representing the same phoneme.

inductive instruction: Instructional procedure that begins with an analysis of specifics from which generalizations are formed; a specific-to-general emphasis.

L1: A learner's primary or first language.

L2: A child or adult who is learning a second language other than the first or native language.

LEP: Limited English proficiency.

macron: An orthographic diacritic symbol (ˉ) placed over a vowel letter to show that it is pronounced as a long sound (sometimes called *glided vowels*).

onset: The consonant sound(s) of a syllable that comes before the vowel sound. (See the definition of *rime* for examples of *onsets.*)

open syllable: Any syllable ending with a vowel phoneme. Examples: see /ē/; may /ā/; boy /oi/; auto /ō/.

phoneme blending: The process of recognizing isolated speech sounds and the ability to pronounce the word for which they stand.

phoneme segmentation: The ability of isolating all the sounds of a word.

phoneme: The smallest *sound* unit of a language that distinguishes one word from another. Examples: The phoneme /h/ distinguishes *hat* from *at;* the words *tell* and *yell* are distinguished by their initial phonemes /t/ and /y/, respectively.

phonemic awareness: The ability to recognize spoken words as a sequence of individual sounds.

phonetics: The scientific study of human speech sounds.

phonics: A method in which basic phonetics, the study of human speech sounds, is used to teach beginning reading.

phonogram: A letter sequence composed of a vowel grapheme and an ending consonant grapheme(s) that represent a sound, such as *-ig* in *wig, dig,* and *big* or *-ack* in *back, tack,* and *sack.* The term was coined by Isaac Pitman in the mid-1800s.

r-controlled vowel: When a vowel letter is followed by the letter *r*, it makes the vowel sound neither long nor short. For example, in *her*, the vowel sound becomes /û/; in *dare*, it becomes /â/.

rime: The part of a syllable that includes the vowel sound and any consonant sound(s) that comes after it. The graphic representation of a rime is referred to as a *phonogram*. For example, in the word *mat*, the onset is /m/, and the rime is /at/.

root: Often used as a synonym for *base word*.

schwa sound: An unstressed vowel sound commonly occurring in unstressed syllables. It is represented by the symbol /ə/, and it closely resembles the short sound for *u*. Examples: *a* in *about; o* in *occur; i* in *pencil; u* in *circus*.

syllable: A unit of pronunciation consisting of a vowel alone or a vowel with one or more consonants. There can be only one vowel phoneme (sound) in each syllable.

synthetic phonics: A part-to-whole phonics approach that emphasizes the learning of individual sounds, often in isolation, and combining them to form words; also known as *explicit phonics*.

TESOL: Teaching English as a Second Language.

umlaut: An orthographic symbol (¨) placed above vowel graphemes to indicate pronunciation.

virgules: A set of slanted lines used in linguistics and the study of phonics to indicate a sound or sounds such as /ā/. In this case, the virgules bracket the long a sound as in the word *hay*.

visual discrimination: The ability to visually perceive similarities and differences; in reading, this refers to the ability to perceive similarities and differences between written letters and words.

vowels: Sounds represented by *a, e, i, o, u,* and sometimes *y* and *w,* in the English alphabet. Vowels are sounds that are made without closing or restricting the breath channel.

References

Adams, M. J. (1990). *Beginning to read: Thinking and learning about print.* Cambridge, MA: MIT Press.

Adamson, P. (2006). Balancing reading and language learning: A resource for teaching english language learners k-5. *School Library Journal, 52,* 91–92.

Anderson, N. (2002). *The role of metacognition in second language teaching and learning.* Washington, DC: Center for Applied Linguistics.

Anderson, R. C., Hiebert, E. H., Scott, J. A., & Wilkinson, I. A. G. (1984). *Becoming a nation of readers: The report of the commission on reading.* Washington, DC: National Institute of Education, U.S. Department of Education.

Arabski, J., & Wojtaszek, A. (Eds.). (2010). *Neurolinguistic and psycholinguistic perspectives in SLA.* Buffalo, NY: Multilingual Matters.

Ashbrook, J. (2010). Learning a "new language": The objective approach to early literacy English. *Educational Psychology in Practice, 26*(3), 219–238.

August, D., & Shanahan, T. (2010). Response to a review on developing literacy in second-language learners: Report of the National Literacy Panel on Language Minority Children and Youth. *Journal of Literacy Research, 42*(3), 341–348.

Bailey, M. H. (1967, February). The utility of phonic generalizations in grades one through six. *The Reading Teacher, 20,* 413–418.

Balmuth, M. (2009). *The roots of phonics: A historical introduction.* Baltimore, MD: Brookes.

Barnyak, N., & Paquette, K. (2010). An investigation of elementary pre-service teachers' reading instructional beliefs. *Reading Improvement, 47*(1), 7–11.

Baron, A. (1999). *The influence of age of learning on syllable structure in the L2 speaker.* University of Ottawa, Canada. AAT MQ52287.

Bear, D., Invernizzi, M., Templeton, S., & Johnston, F. (2004). *Words their way* (3rd ed.). Upper Saddle River, NJ: Pearson.

Beard, R., Myhill, d., Riley, J., & Nystrand, M. (2009). *The SAGE handbook of writing development.* Los Angeles, CA: SAGE.

Beron, K. (2004). Oral language and reading success: A structural equation modeling approach. *Structural Equation Modeling: A Multidisciplinary Journal, 11*(1), 110–131.

Beverly, B., Giles, R., & Buck, K. (2009). First-grade reading gains following enrichment: Phonics plus decodable texts compared to authentic literature read-alouds. *Reading Improvement, 46*(4), 191–205.

Bhatia, T., & Ritchie, W. (2006). *The handbook of bilingualism.* Malden, MA: Blackwell.

Birdsong, D. (1999). *Second language acquisition and the critical period hypothesis.* Mahwah, NJ: Erlbaum.

Blackman, B. A. (1984, August). Relationship of rapid naming ability and language analysis skills to kindergarten and first-grade reading achievement. *Journal of Educational Psychology, 76,* 610–622.

Bond, G. L., & Dykstra, R. (1967). *Final report, project no. X-001.* Washington, DC: Bureau of Research, Office of Education, U.S. Department of Health, Education, and Welfare.

Bond, G. L., Tinker, M. A., Wasson, B. B., & Wasson, J. B. (1989). *Reading difficulties: Their diagnosis and correction* (6th ed.). Upper Saddle River, NJ: Merrill/ Prentice Hall.

Bongaerts, T. (2005). Introduction: Ultimate attainment of the critical period hypothesis for second language acquisition. *IRAL: International Review of Applied Linguistics in Language Teaching, 43*(4), 259–267.

Bowyer-Crane, C., Snowling, M., Duff, F., Fieldsend, E., Carroll, J., Miles, J., Götz, K., & Hulme, C. (2008). Improving early language and literacy skills: Differential effects of an oral language versus a phonology with reading intervention. *Journal of Child Psychology and Psychiatry, 49*(4), 422–432.

Bradley, L., & Bryant, P. E. (1983, February). Categorizing sounds and learning to read—A causal connection. *Nature, 301,* 419–421.

Branum-Martin, L. (2006). Bilingual phonological awareness: Multilevel construction validation among Spanish-speaking kindergarteners in transitional bilingual education classrooms. *Journal of Educational Psychology, 98*(1), 170–181.

Branum-Martin, L., & Foorman, B. (2010). Contextual effects of bilingual programs on beginning reading. *Journal of Educational Psychology, 102*(2), 341–355.

Brice, A. (2002). *The Hispanic child: Speech, language, culture, and education.* Boston, MA: Allyn & Bacon.

Brown, H. D. (2007). *Principles of language learning and teaching.* White Plains, NY: Pearson Education.

Brown, S. (2009). Collaborative inquiry: The quest to improve classroom instruction. *Childhood Education, 86*(2), 105–107.

Burke, M., Hagen-Burke, S., Kwok, O., & Parker, R. (2009). Predictive validity of early literacy indicators from the middle of kindergarten to second grade. *Journal of Special Education, 42*(4), 209–226.

Burmeister, L. E. (1966). *An evaluation of the inductive and deductive group approaches to teaching selected word analysis generalizations to disabled readers in eighth and ninth grade.* Unpublished doctoral dissertation, University of Wisconsin.

Burmeister, L. E. (1968, February). Vowel pairs. *The Reading Teacher, 21,* 445–452.

Byrd, C. (2008). Reading instruction beliefs and practices of early elementary school teachers. *PSI Chi Journal of Undergraduate Research, 13*(2), 76–85.

Caldwell, E. C., Roth, S. R., & Turner, R. R. (1978, Spring). A reconsideration of phonic generalizations. *Journal of Reading Behavior, 10,* 91–96.

Caldwell, J., & Leslie, L. (2005). *Intervention strategies to follow informal reading inventory assessment.* Upper Saddle River, NJ: Pearson.

Calfee, R. C., Lindamood, P., & Lindamood, C. (1973, June). Acoustic-phonetic skills and reading—Kindergarten through twelfth grade. *Journal of Educational Psychology, 64,* 293–298.

Calhoon, B., Otaiba, S., Cihak, D., King, A., & Avalos, A. (2007). Effects of a peer-mediated program on reading skill acquisition for two-way bilingual first-grade classrooms. *Learning Disability Quarterly, 30*(3), 169–184.

Carlo, M., August, D., McLaughlin, B., Snow, C., Lippman, D., & White, C. (2004). Closing the gap: Addressing the vocabulary needs of English language learners in bilingual and mainstream classrooms. *Reading Research Quarterly, 39*(2), 188–215.

Cassady, J., Valadez, C., & Garrett, S. (2010). Literacy trends and issues: A look at the five pillars and the cement that supports them. *The Reading Teacher, 63*(8), 644–655.

Chall, J. (1967). *Learning to read: The great debate.* New York, NY: McGraw-Hill.

Chappell, J. (2008). The link between music and literacy. *Teaching Music, 15*(5), 46.

Chen, Y. (2009). Language support for emergent bilinguals in English mainstream schools: An observational study. *Language and Culture, 22*(1), 57–70.

Cholin, J., & Levelt, W. (2009). Effects of syllable preparation and syllable frequency in speech production: Further evidence for syllabic units at a postlexical level. *Language and Cognitive Processes, 24*(5), 662–684.

Clymer, T. (1963). The utility of phonic generalizations in the primary grades. *The Reading Teacher, 16,* 252–258.

Clymer, T. (1996, November). The utility of phonic generalizations in the primary grades. *The Reading Teacher, 50*(3), 182–187.

Coppola, E., & Primas, E. (2009). *One classroom, many learners: Best literacy practices for today's multilingual classrooms.* Newark, DE: International Reading Association.

Coulter, G. (2009). Oral reading fluency: Accuracy of assessing errors and classification of readers using a 1-min timed reading sample. *Preventing School Failure, 54*(1), 71–76.

Cox, B., & Hopkins, C. (2006). Building on theoretical principles gleaned from Reading Recovery to inform classroom practice. *Reading Research Quarterly, 41*(2), 254–268.

Cox, C., & Boyd-Batstone, P. (2009). *Engaging English learners: Exploring literature, developing literacy, and differentiating instruction.* Boston, MA: Allyn & Bacon.

Cunningham, A., Stanovich, K., & Stanovich, P. (2004). Disciplinary knowledge of k-3 teachers and their knowledge calibration in the doman of early literacy. *Annals of Dyslexia, 54*(1), 139–167.

Cutting, L., Cole, C., Levine, T., & Mahone, E. (2009). Effects of fluency, oral language, and executive function on reading comprehension performance. *Annals of Dyslexia, 59*(1), 34–54.

DeCapua, A., Smathers, W., & Tang, L. (2007). Schooling, interrupted. *Educational Leadership, 64*(6), 40–46.

Deeney, T. A. (2010). One-minute fluency measures: Mixed messages in assessment and instruction. *The Reading Teacher, 63*(6), 440–450.

DelliCarpini, M. (2010). Success with ELLs. *English Journal, 99*(4), 102–104.

Dessoff, A. (2007, August). DIBELS draws doers & doubters: Dynamic Indicators of Basic Early Literacy Skills monitor K6 reading progress but raise questions. *District Administration,* 38–43.

Dilberto, J., Beattie, J., Flowers, C., & Algozzine, R. (2008). Effects of teaching syllable skills instruction on reading achievement in struggling middle school readers. *Literacy Research and Instruction, 48*(1), 1–14.

Domyei, Z. (2009). *The psychology of second language acquisition.* New York, NY: Oxford University Press.

Duffy, G. (2003). *Explaining reading: A resource for teaching concepts, skills, and strategies.* New York, NY: Guilford Press.

Durkin, D. (1993). *Teaching them to read* (6th ed.). Boston, MA: Allyn & Bacon.

Duursma, E., Romero-Contreras, S., Szuber, A., Proctor, P., & Snow, C. (2007). The role of home literacy and language environment on bilinguals' English and Spanish vocabulary development. *Applied Linguistics, 28*(1), 171–190.

Echevarria, J., & Graves, A. (2007). *Sheltered content instruction: Teaching English language learners with diverse abilities.* Boston, MA: Allyn & Bacon.

Edmiaston, R. K. (1984, July/August). Oral language and reading: How are they related for third graders? *Remedial and Special Education, 5,* 33–37.

Ehri, L. C. (1979). *Linguistic insight: Threshold of reading acquisition.* In T. G. Waller & G. E. MacKinnon (Eds.), *Reading research: Advances in theory and practice* (Vol. 1, pp. 63–114). New York, NY: Academic Press.

Ekwall, E. (1976). *Diagnosis and remediation of the disabled reader.* Boston, MA: Allyn & Bacon.

Emans, R. (1967, February). The usefulness of phonic generalizations above the primary grades. *The Reading Teacher, 20,* 419–425.

Emans, R. (1968, May). *History of phonics. Elementary English, 45,* 602–608.

Eslami-Rasekh, Z. (2005). Raising the pragmatic awareness of language learners. *ELT Journal, 59*(3), 199–208.

Fan, M. (2003). Frequency of use, perceived usefulness, and actual usefulness of second language vocabulary strategies: A study of Hong Kong learners. *The Modern Language Journal, 87*(ii), 222–241.

Farrington, P. (2007). A window into the mind: Using miscue analysis. *Literacy Today, 52,* 10–11.

Fawson, P., Ludlow, B., Reutzel, R., Dweeks, R., & Smith, J. (2006). Examining the reliability of running records: Attaining generalizable results. *The Journal of Educational Research, 100*(2), 113–126.

Ferris, A. (2006). Social structure and child poverty. *Social Indicators Research, 78*(3), 453–472.

Flavell, J. (1977). *Cognitive development.* Upper Saddle River, NJ: Merrill/Prentice Hall.

Flesch, R. (1955). *Why Johnny can't read.* New York, NY: Harper Press.

Flynt, E., & Cooter, B. (2004). *Reading inventory for the classroom* (5th ed.). Upper Saddle River, NJ: Pearson.

Fox, B. (2003). *Word recognition activities patterns and strategies for developing fluency.* Upper Saddle River, NJ: Pearson.

Francis, D., & Mehta, P. (2010). Contextual effects of bilingual programs on beginning reading. *Journal of Educational Psychology, 102*(2), 341–355.

Fuld, P. (1968, February). Vowel sounds in VCC words. *The Reading Teacher, 21,* 442–444.

Gabriele, A., Troseth, E., Martohardjono, G., & Otheguy, R. (2009). Emergent literacy skills in bilingual children: Evidence for the role of L1 syntactic comprehension. *International Journal of Bilingual Education and Bilingualism, 12*(5), 533–547.

Gallo, Y., Garcia, M., Pinuelas, L., & Youngs, I. (2008). Crisis in the Southwest: Bilingual education program inconsistencies. *Multicultural Education, 16*(2), 10–16.

Garcia, T. (2007). Facilitating the reading process: A combination approach. *Teaching Exceptional Children, 39*(3), 12.

Gates, L. (1986, Summer). The consonant generalizations revisited. *Reading Horizons, 26,* 232–236.

Genishi, C., & Haas Dyson, A. (2009). *Children language and literacy: Diverse learners in diverse times*. New York, NY: Teachers' College Press.

Gerber, M., Jimenez, T., Leafstedt, J., Villaruz, J., Richards, C., & English, J. (2004). English reading effects of small-group intensive intervention I Spanish k-1 English learners. *Learning Disabilities Research & Practice, 19*(4), 239–251.

German, D., & Newman, R. (2007). Oral reading skills of children with oral language (word finding) difficulties. *Reading Psychology, 28*(5), 387–442.

Gersten, R., & Geva, E. (2003, April). Teaching reading to early language learners. *Educational Leadership*, 6.

Geva, E. (2006). Reading efficiency in native English-speaking and English-as-a-second-language children: The role of oral proficiency and underlying cognitive-linguistic processes. *Scientific Studies of Reading, 10*(1), 31–57.

Goffreda, C., & DiPerna, C. (2010). An empirical review of psychometric evidence for the Dynamic Indicators of Basic Early Literacy Skills. *School Psychology Review, 39*(3), 463–483.

Goh, C. (2008). Metacognitive instruction for second language listening development: Theory, practice and research implications. *RELC Journal, 39*(2), 188–213.

Golinkoff, R. M. (1978). Critique: Phonemic awareness skills and reading achievement. In F. B. Murray & L. L. Pikulski (Eds.), *The acquisition of reading: Cognitive linguistic, and perceptual prerequisites* (pp. 23–41). Baltimore, MD: University Park Press.

Goodman, K. (1969). Analysis of oral reading miscues: Applied psycholinguistics. *Reading Research Quarterly, 5*, 9–30.

Grabner-Hagen, M. (2004). *Exploring differences in spelling strategies used by children* (Doctoral dissertation). Available from ProQuests Dissertations and Theses database. (AAT 3148232)

Graves, A., Plasencia-Peinado, J., Deno, S., & Johnson, J. (2005). Formatively evaluating the reading progress of first-grade English learners in multiple-language classrooms. *Remedial and Special Education, 26*(4), 215–225.

Grinstead, J. (Ed.). (2009). *Hispanic child languages: Typical and impaired development*. Philadelphia, PA: Benjamin.

Groff, P. J. (1984, January). Resolving the letter name controversy. *The Reading Teacher, 37*, 384–388.

Gyovai, L., Cartledge, G., Kourea, L., Yurick, A., & Gibson, L. (2009). Early reading intervention responding to the learning needs of your at-risk English language learners. *Learning Disabilities Quarterly, 32*(3), 143–162.

Hadaway, N., Vardell, S., & Young, T. (2001). Scaffolding oral language development through poetry for students learning English. *The Reading Teacher, 54*(8), 796.

Harris, L. A., & Smith, C. B. (1986). *Reading instruction: Diagnostic teaching in the classroom* (4th ed.). New York, NY: Macmillan.

Heilman, A. W. (1981). *Phonics in proper perspective* (4th ed.). Upper Saddle River, NJ: Merrill/Prentice Hall.

Heilmann, J. (2006). Oral language and reading in bilingual children. *Learning Disabilities Research & Practice, 21*(1), 30–43.

Henning, C., McIntosh, B., Amott, W., & Dodd, B. (2010). Long-term outcome of oral language and phonological awareness intervention with socially disadvantaged preschoolers: The impact on language and literacy. *Journal of Research in Reading, 33*(3), 231–246.

Hillerich, R. L. (1978, April). Reading: Phonics—What about the rules? *Teacher, 95*(8), 94.

Honawar, V. (2009). TEACHER GAP: Training gets boost. *Education Week, 28*(17), 28–29.

Hones, D. F., Aguilar, N, & Thao, S. (2009). La lucha continua: Becoming a bilingual teacher in the era of Praxis II. *Multicultural Education, 16*(3), 18–23.

Houghton Mifflin. (1997a). *Family treasures* (Level 1.5 teacher's ed.). Boston, MA: Author.

Houghton Mifflin. (1997b). *Try it my way* (Level 5 teacher's ed.). Boston, MA: Author.

Houghton Mifflin. (1997c). *Unexpected guests* (Level 1.4 teacher's ed.). Boston, MA: Author.

Huang, J., Cunningham, J., & Finn, A. (2010). Teacher perceptions of ESOL students' greatest challenges in academic English skills: A k-12 perspective. *International Journal of Applied Educational Studies, 8*(1), 68–80.

Huhtala, A., & Lehti-Eklund, H. (2010). Writing a new self in the third place: Language students and identity formation. *Pedagogy, Culture and Society, 18*(3), 273–288.

Jarmulowicz, L. (2006). School-aged children's phonological production of derived English words. *Journal of Speech, Language and Hearing Research, 49*(2), 294–308.

Jarmulowicz, L., & Hay, S. (2009). Derivational morphology: Exploring errors in third graders' productions. *Language, Speech & Hearing Services in Schools, 40*(3), 299–311.

Jedynak, M. (2009). *Critical period hypothesis revisited: The impact of age on ultimate attainment in the pronunciation of a foreign language.* Frankfurt am Main, Germany: Lang.

Jeynes, W. (2008). A meta-analysis of the relationship between phonics instruction and minority elementary school student achievement. *Education and Urban Society, 40*(2), 151–166.

Johns, J. (2009). *Basic reading inventory: Pre-primer through grade twelve and early literacy assessment.* Dubuque, IA: Kendall Hunt.

Johnson, E., Jenkins, J., Yaacov, P., & Catts, H. (2009). How can we improve the accuracy of screening instruments? *Learning Disabilities Research & Practice, 24*(4), 174–185.

Johnston, F. (2001) The utility of phonic generalizations: Let's take another look at Clymer's conclusions. *The Reading Teacher, 55*(2), 132–143.

Jongejan, W., Verhoeven, L., & Siegel, L. (2007). Predictors of reading and spelling abilities in first and second grade language learners. *Journal of Educational Psychology, 99*(4), 835–851.

Joshi, M. (2009a). Do dextbooks used in university reading education courses conform to the instructional recommendations of the National Reading Panel? *Journal of Learning Disabilities, 42*(5), 458–463.

Joshi, M. (2009b). Why elementary teachers might be inadequately prepared to teach reading. *Journal of Learning Disabilities, 42*(5), 392–402.

Kamps, D., Abbott, M., Greenwood, C., Arreaga-Mayer, C., Wills, H., Longstaff, J., Culpepper, M., & Walton, C. (2007). Use of evidence-based small-group reading instruction for English language learners in elementary grades secondary-tier intervention. *Learning Disabilities Quarterly, 30*(3), 153–168.

Kerka, S. (Ed.). (2007). *What works: Evidence-based strategies for youth practitioners.* Columbus: Ohio State University Learning Works Connection.

Kirk, C. J. (2001). *Phonological constraints on the segmentation of continual speech* (Doctoral dissertation. Retrieved from http://scholarworks.umass.edu/dissertations/AAI3027218/

Kroll, A., & De Groot, M.B. (Eds.). (2005). *Handbook of bilingualism: Psycholinguistic approaches.* Oxford, NY: Oxford University Press.

Lane, H., Hudson, R., Leite, W., Kosanovich, M., Strout, M., Fenty, N., & Wright, T. (2009). Teacher knowledge about reading fluency and indicators of students' fluency growth in reading first schools. *Reading & Writing Quarterly, 25*, 57–86.

Langdon, T. (2004). DIBELS: A teacher-friendly basic literacy accountability tool for the primary classroom. *Teaching Exceptional Children, 37*(2), 54.

Leaux, N. (2010). Uneven profiles: Language minority learners' word reading vocabulary, and reading comprehension skills. *Journal of Applied Developmental Psychology, 31*(6), 475–483.

Lems, K. & Soro, T. (Eds). (2010). *Teaching reading to EnglishlLanguage learners: Insights from linguistics.* New York, NY: Guilford Press.

Lesauk, N., Kieffer, M., Faller, E., & Kelly, J. (2010). The effectiveness and ease of implementation of an academic vocabulary intervention for linguistically diverse students in urban middle schools. *Reading Research Quarterly, 45*(2), 196–228.

Lewkowicz, N. K. (1980, October). Phonemic awareness training: What to teach and how to teach it. *Journal of Educational Psychology, 72*, 686–700.

Linan-Thompson, S., Vaughn, S., Prater, K., & Cirino, P. (2006). The response to intervention of English language learners at risk for reading problems. *Journal of Learning Disabilities, 39*(5), 390–398.

Litt, D. (2007). Ten rules for reading. *The Reading Teacher, 60*(6), 570–574.

Long, M. (2005). Problems with supposed counter-evidence to the critical period hypothesis. *IRAL: International Review of Applied Linguistics in Language Teaching, 43*(4), 287–317.

Lugo-Neris, M., Jackson, C., & Goldstein, H. (2010). Effects of a conversation facilitating vocabulary acquisition of young English language learners. *Language Speech and Hearing Services in Schools, 41*(3), 314–327.

Macaro, E. (2006). Strategies for language learning and for language use: Revising the theoretical framework. *The Modern Language Journal, 90*(iii), 320–337.

Malloy, K., Gilbertson, D., & Maxfield, J. (2007). Use of brief experimental analysis for selecting reading interventions for English language learners. *School Psychology Review, 36*(2), 291–310.

Manchon, R. (2009). *Writing in foreign language contexts: Learning, teaching, and research.* Buffalo, NY: Multilingual Matters.

Mann, V. (1994). Phonological skills and the prediction of early reading problems. In N. C. Jordan & J. Goldsmith-Phillips (Eds.), *Learning disabilities: New directions for assessment and intervention.* Needham Heights, MA: Allyn & Bacon.

Manning, M. (2004). Six phonics myths dispelled. *Teaching Pre-K-8, 34*(8), 86–87.

Manyak, P. (2007). A framework for robust literacy instruction for English learners. *The Reading Teacher, 61*(2), 197–200.

Manyak, P. (2008). Explicit code and comprehension instruction for English learners. *The Reading Teacher, 61*(5), 432–434.

Marchand, Y., Adsett, C., & Damper, R. (2009). Automatic syllabification in English: A comparison of different algorithms. *Language and Speech, 52*(1), 1–27.

Mather, N., Sammons, J., & Schwartz, J. (2006). Adaptations of the names test: Easy-to use phonics assessments. *The Reading Teacher, 60*(2), 114–122.

Mattys, S., & Melhorn, J. (2005). How do syllables contribute to the perception of spoken English? Insight from migration paradigm. *Language and Speech, 48*(2), 223–253.

Mayer, C., & Leigh, G. (2010). The changing context for sign bilingual education programs: Issues in language and the development of literacy. *International Journal of Bilingual Education and Bilingualism, 13*(2), 175–186.

McCardle, P., & Chhabra, V. (Eds). (2004). *The voice of evidence in reading research.* Baltimore, MD: Brookes.

McCardle, P., & Hoff, E. (2006). Childhood bilingualism: Research on infancy through school age. Buffalo, NY: Multilingual Matters.

McDonald Connor, C., Son, S., Hindman, A., & Morrison, F. (2005). Teacher qualifications, classroom practices, family characteristics, and preschool experience: Complex effects on first graders' vocabulary and early reading outcomes. *Journal of School Psychology, 43*(4), 343–375.

McIntosh, A., Graves, A., & Gersten, R. (2007). The effects of response to intervention on literacy development in multiple language settings. *Learning Disabilities Quarterly, 30*(3), 197–212.

McKenna, M. (2006). Assessment: Revisiting the role of miscue analysis in effective teaching. *The Reading Teacher, 60*(4), 378.

McMaster, K., Kung, S., Han, I., & Cao, M. (2008). Peer-assisted learning strategies: A "tier 1" approach to promoting English learners' response to intervention. *Exceptional Children, 74*(2), 194–214.

Menken, K., & Kleyn, T. (2010). The long-term impact of subtractive schooling in the educational experiences of secondary English language learners. *International Journal of Bilingual Education & Bilingualism, 13*(4), 399–417.

Meyerson, M., & Kulesza, D. (2002). *Strategies for struggling readers step by step.* Upper Saddle River, NJ: Pearson.

Miller, J., Heilmann, J., Nockerts, A., Iglesias, A., Fabiano, L., & Francis, D. (2006). Oral language in bilingual children. *Learning Disabilities Research & Practice,* (1), 30–43.

Millett, J., Atwill, K., Blanchard, J., & Gorin, J. (2008). The validity of receptive and expressive vocabulary measures with Spanish-speaking kindergarteners learning English. *Reading Psychology, 29*(6), 534–551.

Moats, L. (2000). *Speech to print: Language essentials for teachers.* Baltimore, MD: Brookes.

Moats, L. (2007). *Whole language high jinks: How to tell when "scientifically-based reading instruction" isn't.* Washington, DC: Thomas B. Fordham Foundation.

Moore, R., & Seeger, V. (2010). *Building classroom reading communities: Retrospective miscue analysis and Socratic circles.* Thousand Oaks, CA: Corwin.

Morag, S. (1999). Getting ready for reading: Early phoneme awareness and phonics teaching improves reading and spelling in inner-city second language learners. *British Journal of Educational Psychology, 69*(Part 4), 606.

Morag, S. (2004). Getting ready for reading: A follow-up study of inner-city second language learners at the end of key stage I. *British Journal of Educational Psychology, 74*(Part 1), 15–22.

Nation, A., & Hulme, C. (1997, April–June). Phonemic segmentation, not onset-rime segmentation, predicts early reading and spelling skills. *Reading Research Quarterly, 32,* 154–167.

National Institute of Child Health and Human Development. (2000a). Report of the National Reading Panel. *Teaching children to read: An evidence-based assessment of the scientific research literature on reading and its implications for reading instruction* (NIH Publication No. 00-4769). Washington, DC: U.S. Government Printing Office.

National Institute of Child Health and Human Development. (2000b). Report of the Subgroups of the National Reading Panel. *Teaching children to read: An evidence-based assessment of the scientific research literature on reading and its implications for reading instruction* (NIH Publication No. 00-4754). Washington, DC: U.S. Government Printing Office.

Navarra, J., & Soto-Faraco, S. (2007). Hear lips in a second language: Visual articulatory information enables the perception of second language sounds. *Psychological Research, 71*(1), 4–12.

Nelson, J. (2008). Beyond correlational analysis of the Dynamic Indicators of Basic Early Literacy Skills (DIBELS): A classification validity study. *School Psychology Quarterly, 23*(4), 542–552.

Nikolov, M. (2009). *Early learning of modern foreign languages: Processes and outcomes.* Buffalo, NY: Multilingual Matters.

Ogle, D., & Correa-Kovtun, A. (2010). Supporting English-language learners and struggling readers in content literacy with the "partner reading and content, too" routine. *The Reading Teacher, 63*(7), 532–542.

Ota, M., Hartsuiker, R., & Haywood, S. (2010). Is a FAN always FUN? Phonological and orthographic effects in bilingual visual word recognition. *Language & Speech, 53*(3), 383–403.

Podhajski, B., Mather, N., Nathan, J., & Sammons, J. (2009). Professional development in scientifically based reading instruction. *Journal of Learning Disabilities, 42*(5), 403–417.

Proctor, P., August, D., Carlo, M., & Snow, C. (2005). Native Spanish-speaking children reading in English: Toward a model of comprehension. *Journal of Educational Psychology, 97*(2), 246–256.

Pufpaff, L. (2010). Effects of a 6-week, co-taught literacy unit on pre-service special educators' literacy-education knowledge. *Psychology in the Schools, 47*(5), 493–500.

Restrepo, A., Castilla, A., Schwanenflugel, P., Neuharth-Pritchett, S., & Aroboleda, A. (2010). Effects of a supplemental Spanish oral language program on sentence length, complexity, and grammaticality in Spanish-speaking children attending English-only preschools. *Language Speech & Hearing Services in Schools, 41*(1), 3–13.

Riedel, B., & Samuels, S. J. (2007). The relations between DIBELS, reading comprehension, and vocabulary in urban first-grade students. *Reading Research Quarterly, 42*(4), 546–568.

Rogers, C., & Lopez, A. (2008). Perception of silent-center syllables by native and non-native English speakers. *Acoustical Society of America, 124*(2), 1278–1293.

Rogers, C., DeMasi, T., & Krause, J. (2010). Conventional and clear speech intelligibility of /bVd/ syllables produced by native and non-native English Speakers. *Journal of the Acoustical Society of America, 128*(1), 410–423.

Rosenthal, A. S., Baker, K., & Ginsburg, A. (1983, October). The effects of language background on achievement level and learning among elementary school students. *Sociology of Education, 56,* 157–169.

Roskos, K., Tabors, P., & Lenhart, L. (2009). *Oral language and early literacy in preschool: Talking reading and writing.* Newark, DE: International Reading Association.

Ross, J. (2004). Effects of running records assessment on early literacy achievement. *Journal of Educational Research, 97*(4), 186–194.

Rycik, M. (2007). *Phonics and word identification: Instruction and Intervention, K-8.* Upper Saddle, NJ: Pearson Merrill Prentice Hall.

Santamaria, L. (2009). Culturally responsive differentiated instruction: Narrowing gaps between best pedagogical practices benefiting all learners. *Teachers College Record, 111*(1), 214–247.

Saxton, M. (2010). *Child language: acquisition and development.* Los Angeles, CA: Sage.

Schmitt, M. (2001) The development of children's strategic processing in reading recovery. *Reading Psychology, 22,* 129–151.

Scott, A., & Christ, T. (2009). Curriculum-based measurement of oral reading: Standard errors associated with progressive monitoring outcomes from DIBELS, AIMSweb, and an experiential passage set. *School Psychology Review, 38*(2), 266–283.

Searfoss, L. W., & Readence, J. E. (1994). *Helping children learn to read* (3rd ed.). Boston, MA: Allyn & Bacon.

Seeff-Gabriel, B. (2003). Phonological processing: A platform for assisting second-language learners with English spelling. *Child Language Teaching & Therapy, 19*(3), 291–310.

Shanker, J., & Cockrum, W. (2008). *Locating and correcting reading difficulties* (9th ed.). Boston, MA: Allyn & Bacon.

Shanker, J., & Ekwall, E. (2003). *Locating and correcting reading difficulties* (8th ed.). Upper Saddle River, NJ: Pearson.

Silvaroli, N. J. (1994). *Classroom reading inventory* (7th ed.). Dubuque, IA: Brown & Benchmark.

Silver Burdett Ginn. (1993). *Make a wish* (Level 1.5 teacher's ed.). Needham, MA: Author.

Singleton, D. (1995). A critical look at the critical period hypothesis in second language acquisition. In D. Singleton & Z. Lengtel (Eds.), *The age factor in second language acquisition* (pp. 1–30). Bristol, PA: Multilingual Matters.

Singleton, D. (2005). The critical period hypothesis: A coat of many colors. *IRAL: International Review of Applied Linguistics in Language Teaching, 43*(4), 269–285.

Singleton, D., & Ryan, L. (2004). *Language acquisition: The age factor* (2nd ed.). Buffalo, NY: Clevdon.

Smith, F. (1982). *Understanding reading* (3rd ed.). New York, NY: Holt, Rinehart and Winston.

Smith, K. (2000). *Are cues to syllabification also cues to segmentation?* (Doctoral dissertation). Ohio State University, Columbus.

Smith, S., Scott, K., Roberts, J., & Locke, J. (2008). Disabled readers' performance on tasks of phonological processing, rapid naming and letter knowledge before and after kindergarten. *Learning Disabilities Research & Practice, 23*(3), 113–124.

Snow, C. E., Burns, M. S., & Griffin, P. (Eds.). (1998). *Preventing reading difficulties in young children.* Washington, DC: National Academy Press.

Song, M. J. (2006). Retesting the critical period hypothesis: Is age a strong predictor of ultimate attainment in SLA? *English Teaching, 61*(4), 155–180.

Spache, G. D., & Spache, E. B. (1986). *Reading in the elementary school* (5th ed.). Boston, MA: Allyn & Bacon.

Spache, G. D., Andres, M. C., Curtis, H. A., Rowland, M. L., & Fields, M. H. (1965). *A longitudinal first-grade reading readiness program* (Cooperative Research Project No. 2742). Tallahassee: Florida State Department of Education.

Spear-Swerling, L. (2007). The research-practice divide in beginning reading. *Theory Into Practice, 46*(4), 301–308.

Spear-Swerling, L., & Brucker, P. (2006). Teacher-education students' reading abilities and their knowledge about word structure. *Teacher Education and Special Education, 29*(2), 116–126.

Spear-Swerling, L., Brucker, P., & Alfano, M. (2005). Teachers' literacy-related knowledge and self-perception in relation to preparation and experience. *Annals of Dyslexia, 55*(2), 266–296.

Stahl, S. A., Osborn, J., & Lehr, F. (1990). *Beginning to read: Thinking and learning about print—A summary.* Urbana: Center for the Study of Reading, Reading Research and Education Center, University of Illinois at Urbana-Champaign.

Strickland, D., & Schickedanz, J. (2009). *Learning about print in preschool:Working with letters, words and beginning links with phonemic awareness.* Newark, DE: International Reading Association.

Strid, J., & Booth, J. (2007). The effect of phonological structure on visual word access in bilinguals. *Journal of Psycholinguistic Research, 36,* 383–409.

Stuart, M. (1999). Getting ready for reading: Early phoneme awareness and phonics teaching improves reading and spelling in inner-city second language learners. *British Journal of Educational Psychology, 69,* 587–606.

Sulzby, E., & Teale, W. (1991). *Emergent literacy.* In R. Barr, M. L. Kamil, P. B. Mosenthal, & P. D. Pearson (Eds.), *Handbook of reading research* (Vol. 2, pp. 727–757). New York, NY: Longman.

Swearingen, R., & Allen, D. (2000). *Classroom assessment of reading processes* (2nd ed.). Boston, MA: Houghton Mifflin.

Szczepek, R. (2010). Speech rhythm across turn transitions in cross-cultural talk-in-interaction. *Journal of Pragmatics, 44*(4), 1037–1059.

Tam, B., Heward, W., & Heng, M. (2006). A reading instruction intervention program for English-language learners who are struggling readers. *The Journal of Special Education, 40*(2), 79–93.

Thorndike, E. L., & Lorge, I. (1944). *The teacher's word book of 30,000 words.* New York, NY: Bureau of Publications, Teachers College, Columbia University.

Thu, T. (2010, September). Teaching culture in the EFL/ESL classroom. Paper presented at the Los Angeles Regional California Teachers of English to Speakers of Other Languages, Fullerton, CA.

Tindall, E., & Nisbet, D. (2010). Exploring the essential components of reading. *Journal of Adult Education, 39*(1), 1–9.

Tokuhama-Espinosa, T. (2001). *Raising multilingual children: Foreign language acquisition and children.* Westport, CT: Bergin & Garvey.

Treiman, R., Bowey, J., & Bourassa, D. (2002). Segmentation of spoken words into syllables by English-speaking children as compared to adults. *Journal of Experimental Child Psychology, 83*(3), 213.

Trelease, J. (1995). *The new read-aloud handbook* (3rd ed.). New York, NY: Viking Penguin.

Trelease, J. (2006). *The read-aloud handbook.* New York, NY: Penguin.

Tunmer, W. E., & Nesdale, A. R. (1985, August). Phonemic segmentation skill and beginning reading. *Journal of Educational Psychology, 77,* 417–427.

Vanderwood, M., Linklater, D., & Healy, K. (2008). Predictive accuracy of nonsense word fluency for English language learners. *School Psychology Review, 37*(1), 5–17.

Vaughn, S., Linan-Thompson, S., Mathes, P., Cirano, P., Carlson, C., Pollard-Durodola, S., Cardenas-Hagan, E., & Francis, D. (2006). Effectiveness of Spanish intervention for first-grade English language learners at risk for reading difficulties. *Journal of Learning Disabilities, 39*(1), 56–73.

Verhoeven, L. (2000). Components in early second language reading and spelling. *Scientific Studies in Reading, 4*(4), 313–330.

Walker, B. (2005). *Techniques for reading assessment and instruction.* Upper Saddle River, NJ: Pearson.

Wallace, C. (2007). Vocabulary the key to teaching English language learners to read. *Reading Improvement, 44,* 189–192.

Walqui, A., & Van Lier, L. (2010) *Scaffolding the academic success of adolescent English language learners: A pedagogy of promise.* San Francisco, CA: WestEd.

Wells, G. (2007). Semiotic mediation, dialogue and the construction of knowledge. *Human Development, 50,* 244–274.

Wernham, S. (2005). What is synthetic phonics? *Literacy Today, 44,* 8–9.

Woods, M. L., & Moe, A. J. (2003). *Analytical reading inventory* (7th ed.). Upper Saddle River, NJ: Prentice Hall.

Wurr, A., Theurer, J., & Kim, K. (2008). Retrospective miscue analysis with proficient adult ESL readers. *Journal of Adolescent & Adult Literacy, 52*(4), 324.

Wylie, R. E., & Durrell, D. D. (1970). Teaching vowels through phonograms. *Elementary English, 47,* 787–791.

Yesil-Dagli, U. (2011). Predicting ELL students' beginning first grade English oral reading fluency from initial kindergarten vocabulary, letter naming and phonological awareness skills. *Early Childhood Research Quarterly, 26*(1), 15–29.

Yovanoff, P., Duesbery, L., Alonzo, J., & Tindal, G. (2005). Grade-level invariance of a theoretical casual structure predicting reading comprehension with vocabulary and oral reading fluency. *Educational Measurement: Issues & Practice, 24*(3), 4–12.

Ziegler, J., Grainger, J., & Brysbaert, M. (2010). Modeling word recognition and reading aloud. *European Journal of Cognitive Psychology, 22*(5), 641–649.

Additional Web-Based and Other Resources

Audio Sites
http://www.antimoon.com/how/pronunc-soundsipa.htm

Audio Sites with Links
http://www.sunburstmedia.com/PronWeb.html
http://www.uiowa.edu/~acadtech/phonetics/english/frameset.html
http://dictionary.reference.com/search?q=speech

Center for Applied Linguistics
http://www.cal.org/

Consonant Blends/Digraph Activities
http://www.phonicsworld.com/Consonantblends.html
http://www.tampareads.com/phonics/whereis/index.htm

Consonants
http://evaeaston.com/pr/consonants.html

DIBELS (Dynamic Indicators of Basic Early Literacy Skills) Home Page
http://dibels.uoregon.edu/

Diphthongs
http://www.sadlier-oxford.com/phonics/grade2_3/dipthongs/dipthongs.htm
http://www.celt.stir.ac.uk/staff/HIGDOX/STEPHEN/PHONO/VOWEL/DIPH.HTM

ERIC Linking Site to Educational Information
http://bcol01.ed.gov/CFAPPS/ERIC/resumes/descriptorsummary.
cfm?majordesc=Basal%20Reading

Evaluations of Basal Series
http://www.auburn.edu/~murraba/evaluation.html

Four Blocks
http://teachers.net/gazette/APR03/sigmon.html

General Information on Worldwide Use of Diacritical Marks
http://www.businessballs.com/diacriticalmarks.htm

Great Vowel Shift
http://eweb.furman.edu/~mmenzer/gvs/what.htm

International Phonetic Alphabet
http://www.omniglot.com/writing/ipa.htm
http://www.arts.gla.ac.uk/IPA/ipachart.html

International Reading Association Home Page
http://www.reading.org/

Merriam-Webster Dictionary
http://www.m-w.com

National Council of Teachers of English (NCTE)
http://www.ncte.org/

The Oxford English Dictionary
http://www.oed.com/

Phonograms
http://www.literacyconnections.com/Phonograms.html

http://www.phonogrampage.com/

Resources for Spoken English
http://faculty.washington.edu/dillon/PhonResources/PhonResources.html

Roots and Prefixes
http://www.quia.com/jg/66094.html

http://www.edhelper.com/Word_Roots.htm

http://ancienthistory.about.com/library/weekly/aa052698.htm

Syllabication by Grade-Level Activities
http://www.edhelper.com/language/Syllabication.htm

http://www.createdbyteachers.com/syllablerulescharts.html

http://www.spelling.org/free/syllabication_rules.htm

http://english.glendale.cc.ca.us/SYLLABLES.html

Schwa
http://englishplus.com/grammar/00000383.htm

Schwa Links--Technical
http://www.reference.com/browse/wiki/Schwa

Short Vowel Sounds
http://rbeaudoin333.homestead.com/shortvowel_1.html

http://www.learninghaven.com/la/spelling/short_vowel_sounds.htm

http://www.readingkey.com/phonics/sounds/vowels/voweltest.htm

Sight Word Resources
http://www.fcboe.org/schoolhp/shes/sight_words.htm

http://literacyconnections.com

http://www.createdbyteachers.com

Speech and Special Education
http://parentpals.com/gossamer/pages/Speech_and_Language/
Articulation_and_Phonology/

Speech Articulation
http://academic.gallaudet.edu

Typing Diacritical Marks for Composing Activities in the Classroom
http://www.power-glide.com

HOW TO INSERT DIACRITICAL MARKS INTO YOUR TEACHING DOCUMENTS

Adding special symbols within your teaching materials may be accomplished in several ways, including using a set of special symbols available in the word processing program itself. Another way to insert these special symbols is to use what is called the Unicode system. Most Unicode Internet sites provide differentiated instructions for symbol insertion depending on whether you are using a Mac or a PC. You may find helpful information regarding the Unicode system at: http://unicode.org/standard/WhatIsUnicode.html.

For information regarding The International Phonetic Alphabet (IPA) and its relationship to the phonemes used in English, you may want to visit either or both of the following sites:

http://www.omniglot.com/writing/ipa.htm

http://www.langsci.ucl.ac.uk/ipa/

For information on how to insert special characters for either the Mac or the PC, please visit:

http://www.forlang.wsu.edu/help/keyboards.asp

http://sde.state.ok.us/Curriculum/Bilingual/acronyms.html

EDUCATIONAL RESOURCES AND ORGANIZATIONS

Academic Communication Associates
Features: Academic Communication Associates offers a wide array of teaching materials on its commercial site.

http://www.acadcom.com/ACAwebsite/default.asp

Alta Book Center Publishers
Features: Alta publishes books specifically for the ESL teacher. This is a brief site, but contains helpful titles for the teacher.

http://www.altaesl.com/index.cfm

American Council on the Teaching of Foreign Languages (ACTFL)
Features: ACTFL represents all languages at multiple levels of instruction and the kindergarten through postsecondary teachers and administrators who work in the field of bilingual education. The site also makes reference to proficiency guidelines for language learning.

http://www.actfl.org/i4a/pages/index.cfm?pageid=1

Ballard & Tighe Publishers
Features: Ballard & Tighe offer ESL resources, including an online language proficiency test for preK–12 students.

http://www.ballard-tighe.com/company/news/PR_120110.asp

California Association for Bilingual Education (CABE)
Features: CABE is a nonprofit organization founded in 1976 that represents individuals from diverse cultural, linguistic, and racial backgrounds. The site sets out CABE's vision statement for 21st century educational preparedness for multilingual and multicultural education.

http://www.bilingualeducation.org/about_cabe.php

Center for Applied Linguistics (CAL)
Features: One of the most approachable and helpful sources for language-related materials, including linguistics and psycholinguistic sources.

http://www.cal.org/

The Council for Exceptional Children (CEC)
Features: The CEC supports teachers, parents, and children with special needs and provides invaluable assistance in researching and gathering legislative information for its members.

http://www.cec.sped.org//AM/Template.cfm?Section=Home

Dictionary.com
Features: This free dictionary resource is a valuable reference and research tool for busy educators. Simple to use, it is particularly helpful for teachers working to standardize pronunciation within teaching materials used in reading instruction.

www.dictionary.com

Edmonton Chinese Bilingual Education Association (ECBEA)
Features: The chief purpose of ECBEA is to promote Chinese language and culture, but the framework of its support system for parents and learners with the Edmonton Public Schools offers a model for other districts to follow regardless of the language base of their ESL students. It also offers an example within bilingual education called less commonly taught languages (LCTL). Membership in ECBEA is limited to parents and students. Address: Edmonton Chinese Bilingual Education Association

Box 220, #21-10405 Jasper Avenue Edmonton, Alberta

T5J 3S2

http://www.ecbea.org/about.php

Harvard Graduate School of Education
Features: An excellent source for diverse topics in education, including reading and bilingual education and topics related to teaching. This is a large hub site with numerous helpful web links.

http://www.gse.harvard.edu/library/educator_resources.html

Houghton Mifflin Harcourt
Features: A long-term publisher of educational materials in reading, Houghton Mifflin Harcourt remains one of the leaders in the field. Its website is both approachable and helpful.

http://customercare.hmhco.com/index.html

John Benjamins Publishing Company
Features: Benjamins Publishing Company offers professional development materials and texts helpful to educators, including books in Spanish.

http://www.benjamins.nl

Lectorum Publications, Inc.
Features: Children's books in Spanish as well as a bilingual format for both English and Spanish teachers and other educators.

http://www.lectorum.com

Lee & Low Books
Features: Offers a rich array of bilingual curriculum materials and other materials helpful to educators.

http://www.leeandlow.com

McGraw-Hill
Features: Read-alongs and multicultural literature.

www.mcgraw-hill.com

National Clearinghouse for Bilingual Education (NCBE)
Features: NCBE is part of the U.S. Department of Education and is a related to the Office of English Language Acquisition (OELA).

http://www.ncela.gwu.edu/

The National Association of Multicultural Education (NAME)
Features: NAME addresses social and cultural issues facing teachers and others involved in promoting social justice. Its membership comprises members from all over the world, making its concerns truly global. NAME is a rich resource for teachers working in all fields of education.

http://nameorg.org/

The National Coalition for Parent Involvement in Education (NCPIE)
Features: Associated with the Alexandria, Virginia, Public Schools, NCPIE offers rich resources to parents, students, and teachers. Its proximity to Washington, D.C., and many other national organization such as the Council for Exceptional Children and the National Association of Multicultural Education positions the organization well to be aware of changes in educational policy from the U.S. Department of Education.

http://www.ncpie.org/AboutNCPIE/GovernmentAgencies.cfm

National Teacher Education Center (NTEC)
Features: The NTEC site contains helpful information about certification in bilingual education and other useful information for currently certified teachers or those who want to recertify in bilingual education. It is a hub site.

http://www.teach.us/index.php/teaching-bilingual-or-esl.html

Office of English Language Acquisition (OELA)
Features: OELA is a component of the U.S. Department of Education. As its name implies, it offers resources related to English language acquisition and current links to legislation related to English language learning.

http://www2.ed.gov/about/offices/list/oela/index.html

State of New Jersey Department of Education
Features: This hub site contains links to helpful resources related to bilingual education both inside and outside of New Jersey. It offers excellent documentation of the state's response to the needs of bilingual students and support for bilingual education.

http://www.state.nj.us/education/bilingual/resources/websites/orgs.htm

Starfall
Features: Helpful resources to both classroom teachers and school administrators. It is a popular site with graduate students in reading and bilingual education.

www.starfall.com

TeAchnology
Features: Free lesson plans, worksheets and rubrics, and helpful resources for the bilingual classroom.

Web address: http://www.teach-nology.com/

U.S. Department of Education
Features: This hub link includes convenient searchable windows to help narrow topics of interest related to education at the national level.

http://www.ed.gov/

The Teacher Center.org
Features: The Teacher Center contains regional links to the south and eastern regions of the United States. This hub site connects to many resources.

http://www.theteachercenter.org/NewTeacher/GeneralInfo/bilingual_education.asp

ADDITIONAL REFERENCES FOR
FURTHER READING AND STUDY

Hickok, J. (2005). ESL (English as a second language) web sites: Resources for library administrators, librarians, and ESL library users. *Journal of Library Administration, 43*(3/4), 247–262.

Hinkel, E. (Ed.). (2008). *Handbook of research in second language teaching and learning.* New York, NY: Rutledge.

Logan, S., & Johnston, R. (2010). Investigating gender differences in reading. *Educational Review, 62*(2), 175–187.

Manchon, R. (2009). *Writing in foreign language contexts: Learning, teaching, and research.* Buffalo, NY: Multilingual Matters.

McCormick, R., & Pasgurelli, L. (2010). *Teaching reading: Strategies and resources for grades k-6.* New York, NY: Guilford Press.

Morrow, L., Rueda, R., & Lapp, D. (Eds.). (2009). *Handbook of research on literacy and diversity.* New York, NY: Guilford Press.

Orosco, M., & Klingner, J. (2010). One school's implementation of RTI with English language learners: Referring into RTI. *Journal of Learning Disabilities, 43*(3), 269–288.

Ostergaard, L., Ludwig, J., & Nugent, J. (2009). *Transforming English studies: New voices in an emerging genre.* West Lafayette, IN: Parlor Press.

Pacheco, M. (2010). English-language learners' reading achievement: Dialectical relationships between policy and practice in meaning-making opportunities. *Reading Research Quarterly, 45*(3), 292–317.

Rouse, H. (2006). Validity of the dynamic indicators for basic early literacy skills as an indicator of early literacy for urban kindergarten children. *School Psychology Review, 35*(1), 341–355.

Rowlands, K. (2010). Readicide: How schools are killing reading and what you can do about it. *English Journal* (High School Edition), *100*(1), 123–126.

Samson, J., &Lesaux, N. (2009). Language-minority learners in special education: Rates and predictors of identification for services. *Journal of Learning Disabilities, 42*(2), 148–162.

Sanders, P. (2006). Para-educator–supplemental instruction in structural analysis with text reading practices for second and third graders at risk for reading problems. *Remedial and Special Education, 27*(6), 365–378.

Slavin, R., Cheung, A., Groff, C., & Lake, C. (2008). Effective reading programs for middle schools: A best-evidence synthesis. *Reading Research Quarterly, 43*(3), 290–322.

Smith, K. (2000). *Are cues to syllabification also cues to segmentation?* (Doctoral dissertation). Ohio State University, Columbus.

Spear-Swerling, L., & Brucker, P. (2004). Preparing novice teachers to develop basic reading and spelling skills. *Annals of Dyslexia, 54*(2), 332–364.

Sturtevant, E., & Linek, W. (2003). The instructional beliefs and decisions of middle and secondary teachers who successfully blend literacy and content. *Reading Research and Instruction, 43*(1), 74.

Yurick, A., Robinson, P., Carledge, G., Lo, Y., & Evans, T. (2006). Using peer-mediated repeated readings as a fluency-building activity for urban learners. *Education and Treatment of Children, 29*(3), 469–506.